# THE NEW CASSEROLE

Macmillan • USA

# OTHER BOOKS BY FAYE LEVY

*Thirty Low-Fat Meals in 30 Minutes*
*Thirty Low-Fat Vegetarian Meals in 30 Minutes*
*The Low-Fat Jewish Cookbook*
*Faye Levy's International Vegetable Cookbook*
*Faye Levy's International Chicken Cookbook*
*Faye Levy's International Jewish Cookbook*
*Sensational Chocolate*
*Sensational Pasta*
*Fresh from France: Vegetable Creations*
*Fresh from France: Dinner Inspirations*
*Fresh from France: Dessert Sensations*
*Classic Cooking Techniques*
*La Cuisine du Poisson* (in French, with Fernand Chambrette)
*Faye Levy's Favorite Recipes* (in Hebrew)
*French Cooking Without Meat* (in Hebrew)
*French Desserts* (in Hebrew)
*French Cakes, Pastries and Cookies* (in Hebrew)
*The La Varenne Tour Book*

# THE NEW CASSEROLE

## Faye Levy

Macmillan • USA

**MACMILLAN**

A Simon & Schuster Macmillan Company

1633 Broadway

New York, NY 10019-6785

Copyright © 1997 by Faye Levy

Illustrations copyright © Rachael McBrearty

MACMILLAN is a registered trademark of Macmillan, Inc.

Library of Congress Cataloging-in-Publication Data

Levy, Faye.

The new casserole / Faye Levy.

p.   cm.

Includes index.

ISBN 0-02-860993-X (alk. paper)

1. Casserole cookery. 2. Cookery, International. I. Title.

TX693.L68   1997                      97-6059

641.8'21—dc21                         CIP

ISBN: 0-02-860993-X

Manufactured in the United States of America

10 9 8 7 6 5 4 3 2 1

Book Design by Rachael McBrearty—Madhouse Productions

# DEDICATION

For my mother, Pauline Kahn Luria,
and my mentor, Parisian Chef Fernand Chambrette

# CONTENTS

# ACKNOWLEDGMENTS

I am grateful to my editor, Amy Gordon, for making the process of transforming my manuscript into this book a pleasant experience. Thanks also to production editor Denise Hawkins Coursey, to Rachael McBrearty for her design and illustration, to Iris Jeromnimon for designing the cover, and to Lisa Koenig for the cover photo.

A special thanks to those who contributed to my culinary education, especially Fernand Chambrette, Anne Willan, Albert Jorant and Claude Vauguet in France, and Ruth Sirkis in Israel. Thanks also to Maureen and Eric Lasher for their encouragement.

# INTRODUCTION

Many of us grew up with casseroles. Often they were baked mixtures of canned mushroom soup, macaroni, and sometimes tuna, topped with crushed potato chips and processed American cheese. You wouldn't exactly call these old-fashioned dishes elegant, light, or bursting with flavor, but we loved them anyway. My personal favorite was macaroni and cheese.

Contemporary casseroles are different. In contrast to fifties-style baked dinners, they are made of fresh ingredients. Today's casseroles require minimal preparation but have plenty of taste because they are infused with flavors from around the world.

Casseroles are practical nowadays for the same reasons that made them popular in the old days: They simplify meal planning for family suppers; they are often one-pot meals and can be made ahead and reheated (some even improve on reheating); and they are ideal for entertaining and for potluck dinners.

Although I still love macaroni and cheese, now I add cooked fresh asparagus, sautéed mushrooms, roasted peppers, or chiles. Usually I make the béchamel sauce, a savory white sauce, leaner and more highly seasoned by using low-fat milk and adding a generous amount of freshly grated nutmeg and a hint of cayenne pepper. I go easy on the cheese, too. When I use a flavorful cheese like Parmigiano-Reggiano instead of a bland Jack cheese, I can add a smaller quantity, so there is more taste with less fat.

Moving a step further from the original macaroni-and-cheese formula, I sometimes like to add crabmeat or shrimp and omit the cheese. And I do not limit myself to macaroni.

I use flavored pastas such as lemon-seasoned noodles, which taste great with the seafood. Instead of a white sauce, I might make a velouté sauce of stock thickened with a quick roux of flour and butter, or a tomato sauce seasoned with curry and ginger. So, to the delight of my family, I serve a delicious new casserole of lemon noodles with crab and curry-ginger sauce, which evolved from the simple macaroni-and-cheese recipe and is much lower in fat.

In a similar way, we now give new spirit to countless other classic casseroles: Italian lasagnas, French gratins and cassoulets, Hungarian noodle puddings, English shepherd's pies, Spanish paellas, Louisiana jambalayas, Jewish kugels, and Greek moussakas. There are many other casseroles less well known to Americans: Mexican *chilaquiles*, tortillas layered with savory meats, cheese, and chiles; aromatic Moroccan *tajines* of fish, meat, or poultry baked with vegetables or fruit; Provençal baked vegetable *tians*, redolent of onions and garlic; Romanian *givetch* made of many vegetables; and sumptuous Iranian layered casseroles of saffron rice and meats.

Each of these specialties represents a whole family of dishes and can be varied in numerous ways to create new casseroles. We have many more vegetables, fresh herbs, spices, ethnic ingredients, and other flavorings available to us than ever before to help us prepare delectable dishes. We can add zip to lasagna by mixing a chunky Mexican salsa with the filling ingredients, or prepare a light vegetarian cassoulet by substituting shiitake mushrooms for the meat. And we can introduce a new flavor dimension to the familiar broccoli gratin by incorporating a layer of mushroom duxelles.

The broad definition of a casserole is food that is cooked in a "casserole," which can be made of glass, earthenware, enamel-coated cast iron, or other materials. These range from common Pyrex™ baking dishes to deep enamel Dutch ovens to shallow gratin dishes to individual ramekins or soufflé dishes. They can be round, oval, oblong, or square.

Today casseroles are generally baked in the oven, but historically they were sometimes steamed. You can make quick stovetop recipes in a skillet or saucepan, or for even faster versions, cook them in the microwave.

Since many casseroles start with cooked meat or vegetables, they are a great way to use leftovers, from extra Thanksgiving turkey to steamed broccoli florets or grilled peppers you might have on hand. By combining bits of meat and vegetables with grains or pasta, you can create a substantial whole meal in one dish.

We tend to think of casseroles as main courses, but there are also side dish and even dessert renditions, such as Apple-Apricot Noodle Pudding with Cinnamon and Ginger (page 146). Casseroles can be festive for holidays or simple for everyday cooking. They can appear in many forms: as mixtures or in layers, moistened with sauce, broth, or olive oil, topped with a crunchy crust or a fluffy layer of mashed potatoes. One reason that casseroles are so well suited to entertaining is that they hold a certain element of surprise. Your guests don't always know what flavors they will discover under the crust or the top layer of bubbling sauce.

Casseroles are convenient to serve, even to large groups, because no carving is necessary. The food keeps hot in the dish until each person has a helping on his or her plate. And as an added plus, many baking dishes are attractive and make the casserole even more appealing when brought to the table or presented buffet-style.

Practicality is not the only advantage of a casserole. The ingredient flavors complement and enhance each other from being baked together. For example, when you bake chicken with rice and a Latin American *sofrito* of peppers and herbs, the chicken and peppers give the rice a terrific taste.

An excellent choice for meals with the whole family, casseroles will even find fans among the children. These hearty, satisfying one-dish meals are traditional in home cooking. They are easy to make in any kitchen, as they involve no tricky techniques.

By providing a good way to stretch expensive meat and seafood, the casserole not only is economical but also makes nutritional sense. We can use a small amount of meat for flavor, while preparing the bulk of the casserole from pasta, grains, dried beans, or vegetables. Casseroles can easily fit in with nutritionists' recommendations that we eat more grains, legumes, and vegetables, and less meat. By giving us a gratifying way to introduce more vegetables into our menus, casseroles can help us conform to the dietary guidelines in the USDA Food Guide Pyramid.

For our casseroles for the new millennium, I have kept health in mind and have included many low-fat recipes. It's not necessary to make casseroles laden with heavy cheeses and cream. Many prized casseroles, especially those seasoned with Mediterranean and Asian flavors, are appetizing without dairy products. Even in traditional American casseroles the amount of fat can be reduced while keeping the casserole's creamy character. By using common sense and moderation, we can make delicious casseroles that are healthful, too. Good taste and sound nutrition can go hand in hand.

In developing the recipes, I have considered ease of preparation so that many of the dishes can be quickly assembled. I find the casseroles to be fun to prepare, to serve, and to eat, and I hope you will enjoy them as much as I do.

# Ingredients and Techniques

Casseroles are simple to assemble and bake, but here are some tips to make creating casseroles even easier.

## Ingredients to Keep on Hand

The following list includes many foods that are useful for making casseroles. I keep some on hand in the cupboard, some in the refrigerator, and some in the freezer.

### In the Pantry

Dried pasta of several shapes, especially medium noodles and short pastas like shells, spirals, macaroni, orzo, and couscous

Flavored dried pasta, such as lemon, garlic, and hot pepper

Rice of several types: long-grain white and brown, basmati, quick-cooking brown rice

Grains such as barley, bulgur wheat, and buckwheat

Bread crumbs

Onions, garlic, and potatoes

Sun-dried tomatoes, both dry-packed and in olive oil

Dried mushrooms

Dried chiles

Dried beans and lentils

Bottled roasted peppers

Canned beans: white, black, pinto, chickpeas

Canned corn kernels

Canned tomatoes, whole and diced

Canned Chinese vegetables: straw mushrooms, water chestnuts, and baby corn

Canned tomato sauce

Canned tuna and salmon

Canned broth, especially chicken and vegetable

Olive oil, vegetable oil, and sesame oil

Olives

Soy sauce, hoisin sauce, and plum sauce

Mustard and ketchup

Salsa and hot sauce

Dried herbs and spices

### In the Refrigerator

Butter or margarine

Grated Parmesan cheese

Sour cream: regular, low-fat, or nonfat

Carrots

Lemons and oranges

### In the Freezer

Nuts (they stay fresh)

Frozen tortellini and other stuffed pastas

Frozen vegetables: corn, spinach, cauliflower, diced onions, baby onions, bell pepper strips, mixed vegetables

Frozen legumes: lima beans, black-eyed peas, green peas

Use this list as a starting point for stocking your kitchen. If your family loves Roquefort, feta cheese, or sausages, you'll probably have them on hand and can use them to flavor your casseroles.

## Tips on Reheating Casseroles

When you want to reheat part of a casserole, transfer it to another dish in which it will just fit, then place in the oven or microwave to reheat. If you try to reheat it in a half-empty casserole, the dish will burn in the oven. In the microwave, the casserole will not heat evenly. If you're reheating part of a casserole in the oven, oil or butter the new casserole dish before transferring the food to it.

## Homemade Techniques

When peppers, tomatoes, and artichokes are plentiful, prepare them fresh when making casseroles. When they are not in season, you can substitute roasted peppers in jars, canned, peeled tomatoes, and frozen or canned artichoke hearts.

# Grilled or Roasted Bell Peppers

**Whole red or green bell peppers**

*When you're grilling food, it's a good idea to put a few bell peppers on the barbecue so you'll have homemade roasted peppers. They're terrific for flavoring all sorts of casseroles, whether they're made of rice, pasta, fish, or chicken. They also make a delectable accompaniment.*

Preheat the barbecue or broiler. Put the peppers on a rack about 4 inches from the heat. Broil, turning every 4 to 5 minutes with tongs, until the skins are blistered and charred, 15 to 20 minutes total. Or char the peppers over a gas burner, turning often with tongs, until the skins blacken, about 5 minutes.

Transfer to a bowl and cover tightly, or put in a bag and close tightly. Let stand 10 minutes. When the peppers are cool enough to handle, peel with a paring knife but do not rinse. Halve the peppers, being careful, as there may be hot liquid inside. Discard the pepper tops, seeds, and ribs. Cut the peppers into wide strips or dice for adding to casseroles. Will keep up to 5 days in the refrigerator.

# Peeled and Seeded Tomatoes

**Whole tomatoes**

Removing the peel and seeds of tomatoes is a basic step in making tomato sauces for many casseroles.

Cut the cores from the tomatoes. Turn the tomatoes over and use a sharp knife to slit the skin in an X-shaped cut.

In a saucepan filled with enough boiling water to cover generously, boil the tomatoes until the skin begins to pull away from the flesh near each cut, about 10 seconds. With a slotted spoon, remove the tomatoes and put in a bowl of cold water. Let sit for a few seconds.

Remove the tomatoes from the water and pull off the skins with a paring knife. Halve the tomatoes crosswise. Hold each half over a bowl, cut side down, and squeeze to remove the seeds.

# Artichoke Hearts

**2 lemons, halved**
**4 artichokes**
**Salt**

Fresh artichoke hearts have a much better taste and texture than canned or frozen. When artichokes are in season, prepare Vegetarian Paella (page 42) using fresh artichoke hearts. They're also great in poultry or pasta casseroles.

*Makes 4 artichoke hearts*

Into a bowl of cold water, squeeze the juice of 1½ lemons. Break off the stem of 1 artichoke and remove the large leaves at the bottom. Put the artichoke on its side on a cutting board. Using a sharp knife, cut off the lower circle of leaves up to the edge of the artichoke heart; turn the artichoke slightly after each cut. Rub the cut edges with lemon. Cut off the leaves under the base. Trim the base, removing all the dark green areas. Rub again with lemon. Cut off the central cone of leaves just above the heart. Put the artichoke in the bowl of lemon water. Prepare the remaining artichokes in the same way. Keep the artichokes in lemon water until ready to cook.

To cook the artichoke hearts: To a medium saucepan of boiling salted water, add 1 tablespoon lemon juice. Add the artichokes. Cover and simmer over low heat until tender when pierced with a knife, 15 to 20 minutes. Cool to lukewarm in the liquid. Using a teaspoon, scoop out the hairlike "choke" from the center of each artichoke.

# Chicken and Turkey Casseroles

*Chicken Casserole with Tomatoes and Middle Eastern Spices*

*Chicken Baked with Caribbean Sofrito and Rice*

*Chicken en Cocotte with Asparagus, Shrimp, and Tarragon*

*Chicken Noodle Casserole with Mustard Sauce and Vegetable Julienne*

*Mango Chicken with Macadamia Nuts, Orzo, and Green Onions*

*Cumin-Scented Chicken Baked with Onion Rice*

*Turkey and Corn Casserole with Olives and Raisins*

Does it happen to you too, that you end up with leftover barbecued or roasted chicken? Perhaps you wanted to make sure there was plenty of food for your guests, so you put too much meat on the grill or in the oven. Or maybe you bought large quantities of chicken pieces advertised at a great price at the market and grilled or roasted them, thinking it would be nice to have extra cooked chicken on hand.

Let's face it, reheated portions of barbecued or roasted poultry are not so tempting, whether you warm them in the microwave or in the oven. Instead, combine them with pasta or rice to make a satisfying, convenient, economical casserole. This type of entrée is a long-standing American tradition. Preparing a casserole is a popular way to use up leftover Thanksgiving turkey, often mixing the meat with extra cooked vegetables, moistened with a little turkey gravy. Cooked chicken baked with noodles and white sauce is

1

another time-honored specialty. Casseroles are also used to give new interest to poached poultry or even chicken that has been simmered at length to make soup.

Yet poultry casseroles are much more than mere ways to use extra cooked chicken or turkey. Baking in a casserole is also an excellent technique for cooking chicken pieces. They make fabulous entrées when baked with beans, potatoes, or rice because the chicken juices flavor these foods, as in Provençal Chicken with White Beans, Tomatoes, and Thyme (page 137).

For these casseroles you can use any chicken pieces you like: breast pieces for a lighter entrée, leg or thigh pieces for a richer dish, or some of each to please everyone. Use boneless chicken breasts or thighs for quick-cooking dishes such as Sweet-and-Sour Apricot Chicken (page 121).

Ground chicken and turkey cook rapidly and make terrific casseroles when combined with corn, olives, and raisins, for example, to make a Latin American–style entrée. In the interest of low-fat cooking, ground chicken and turkey can be substituted for beef in your family's favorite dishes. For an especially lean casserole, you can buy ground turkey breast.

Flavorings have come a long way from the old-fashioned white sauce. Middle Eastern seasonings perk up chicken pieces in Cumin-Scented Chicken Baked with Onion Rice. The warm flavors of sautéed peppers lend a tasty touch to Chicken Baked with Caribbean Sofrito and Rice. Fruit complements the chicken in Mango Chicken with Macadamia Nuts, Orzo, and Green Onions, a delightful savory and sweet casserole.

If you don't have time to cook chicken and have no cooked chicken or turkey on hand, there are plenty of convenience foods, such as prepared roasted turkey or chicken, smoked turkey, and turkey pastrami, that you can turn into quick casseroles. Use turkey or chicken sausages for a leaner alternative to those made with beef or pork. Combine them with pasta, rice, or vegetables to make effortless entrées, such as Spinach and Sausage Casserole with Brown Rice (page 101). With so many possibilities for making delicious casseroles from poultry with vegetables, grains, and flavorings, you're sure to find a variety of recipes your family will enjoy.

# Chicken Casserole with Tomatoes and Middle Eastern Spices

*This worked well for a church pot luck.*

**2 tablespoons olive oil**

**1 large onion, coarsely chopped**

**8 large cloves garlic, chopped**

**4 teaspoons ground cumin**

**2 teaspoons ground coriander**

**1/2 teaspoon sweet paprika**

**1/2 teaspoon turmeric**

**1/4 teaspoon cayenne pepper, or to taste**

**Salt and freshly ground black pepper**

**One 14 1/2-ounce can diced tomatoes, drained**

**1 tablespoon tomato paste**

**1/2 cup water**

**6 pounds chicken pieces**

For this easy-to-make casserole, the chicken pieces bake in an aromatic mixture of tomatoes, garlic, cumin, coriander, and turmeric. These seasonings are popular among Sephardic Jews in Israel. They also reign supreme among cooks in Morocco when creating their sumptuous casseroles known as tajines. The chicken gains a wonderful flavor and color from the sauce that forms during baking.

*Makes 8 servings*

Preheat the oven to 400°F. In a large skillet, heat the oil over medium-low heat. Add the onion and sauté until golden, about 7 minutes. Remove from the heat. Stir in the garlic, cumin, coriander, paprika, turmeric, cayenne, salt and black pepper to taste, tomatoes, tomato paste, and 1/4 cup of the water, and set aside.

Season the chicken pieces with salt and place in a large, shallow roasting pan. Add the tomato-spice mixture from the skillet and stir to coat the chicken thoroughly. Turn the chicken pieces skin side down. Cover the pan with foil and bake 30 minutes. Uncover, turn the pieces skin side up, and bake 15 minutes.

Add the remaining 1/4 cup water to the pan. Continue baking the chicken, basting once, 20 to 30 minutes longer or until it is tender and its juices run clear when the thickest part of the thigh is pierced with a sharp knife. Serve hot.

*\* I browned the chicken first.*

# Chicken Baked with Caribbean Sofrito and Rice

2 tablespoons olive oil

2½ pounds chicken pieces, patted dry

Salt and freshly ground black pepper

2 medium onions, chopped

1 red bell pepper, diced

1 yellow or red bell pepper, diced

1 green bell pepper, diced

4 large cloves garlic, minced

¼ cup chopped cilantro, plus extra for garnish

½ pound ripe tomatoes, peeled, seeded (see page xviii), and diced, or one 14½-ounce can diced tomatoes, drained

3 cups chicken stock (page 157), or one 14½-ounce can broth mixed with 1¼ cups water

1½ cups white rice, preferably short-grain

1 tablespoon chopped fresh oregano, or 1 teaspoon dried

I n Spain, sofrito *usually refers to a flavoring medley of sautéed onions, garlic, and tomatoes and resembles a thick, chunky tomato sauce. The Spanish brought their* sofrito *to the New World, where it became popular in the Caribbean Islands, especially Cuba and Puerto Rico. Although the name remained the same, the recipe evolved. Peppers were added, usually sweet, sometimes hot. In some versions cilantro was included. Tomatoes became less prominent and sometimes were omitted altogether.*

*Today Caribbean cooks put this popular medley of aromatic vegetables in the pot as a matter of course when they begin to cook almost anything—chicken, meat, fish, beans, rice, sauces, stews, and soups.*

*In this casserole, the sofrito has more bell peppers than usual, and in several colors, so the peppers are more than just a flavoring and play the role of vegetable as well. The high proportion of vegetables, along with the cilantro and oregano, give this meal-in-one-pot a lively taste.*

*For even cooking, the casserole begins on top of the stove. The chicken, sauce, and rice finish cooking together in the oven. Use a casserole that is stainless steel or enamel-lined cast iron and can be used for stovetop cooking as well as oven baking.*

*Makes 4 servings*

In a wide ovenproof casserole or Dutch oven, heat the oil over medium heat. Add the chicken pieces in batches, sprinkle with salt and pepper to taste, and brown on all sides. Remove the chicken pieces to a plate as they brown.

For the *sofrito*: Pour off all but 2 tablespoons fat from the pan. Add the onions and all of the peppers and sauté over medium-low heat, stirring often, until the onions turn golden, about 7 minutes. Stir in the garlic and cilantro and sauté 1 minute. Add the tomatoes and cook over medium heat for 2 minutes.

Preheat the oven to 375°F. Add the stock and bring to a simmer. Return the chicken pieces to the pan, cover with a lid, and simmer over low heat for 30 minutes.

Stir the rice and oregano into the cooking liquid. Cover and transfer to the oven. Bake about 30 minutes, or until the chicken and rice are tender. Let stand, covered, 10 minutes before serving. Serve sprinkled with cilantro.

# Chicken en Cocotte with Asparagus, Shrimp, and Tarragon

3½-pound chicken, giblets and fat removed, patted dry

Salt and freshly ground black pepper

3 sprigs fresh tarragon

2 tablespoons vegetable oil

1 tablespoon butter or additional vegetable oil

¾ to 1 pound asparagus spears, peeled if thick, cut into 2- to 3-inch lengths

¼ cup dry white wine

¼ cup chicken stock (page 157) or broth

¼ pound medium shrimp, shelled and deveined

1 tablespoon minced fresh tarragon

1 tablespoon minced fresh Italian parsley

2 teaspoons fresh lemon juice

*The addition of asparagus and shrimp turn the French classic chicken with tarragon into a beautiful dish. The chicken is baked "en cocotte," one of France's favorite ways to cook chicken, which is also known as cooking "en casserole." The chicken bakes whole in a casserole and comes out juicy and delicious, with a tasty sauce. I like to add the shrimp and asparagus after the chicken is baked because their cooking time is very brief.*

*Makes 4 servings*

Preheat the oven to 400°F. Sprinkle the chicken evenly with salt and pepper on all sides and inside. Put the tarragon sprigs inside the chicken. Truss the chicken if desired.

In a heavy, 4- to 5-quart, enamel-lined, cast-iron casserole, heat the oil and butter over medium-high heat. Set the chicken in the casserole on its side. Cover with a large spatter screen if desired, and brown the side of the chicken, about 3 minutes; reduce the heat if the fat becomes too dark. Using 2 wooden spoons, gently turn the chicken on its breast and brown for about 3 minutes. Turn the chicken on its other side and brown 3 more minutes. Turn the chicken on its back and brown for 2 minutes.

Baste the chicken with the pan juices. Cover the casserole with a lid and bake the chicken in the oven for about 35 minutes, or until its juices run clear when the thickest part of the leg is pierced with a thin knife or skewer; if the juices are pink, bake a few more minutes and test again. (The chicken can be kept warm in the casserole, covered, for 15 minutes.)

In a medium saucepan of boiling salted water, cook the asparagus until barely tender, about 2 minutes. Drain, rinse with cold water, and drain well.

Transfer the chicken to a cutting board, reserving the juices in the casserole. Discard the trussing strings if used. Carve into 4 pieces. Cover the chicken with foil and keep it warm.

Skim as much fat as possible from the juices in the casserole. Return to the stovetop over high heat and bring the juices to a boil. Add the wine and stock and bring to a boil, skimming off the fat frequently. Boil until reduced by half, about 2 minutes. Add the shrimp and asparagus and cook over low heat, stirring, until the shrimp turn pink, about 2 minutes. Remove from the heat and add the tarragon, parsley, and lemon juice. Taste and adjust the seasonings.

Return the chicken to the casserole. Spoon the shrimp and asparagus mixture over the chicken pieces and serve.

# Chicken Noodle Casserole with Mustard Sauce and Vegetable Julienne

8 ounces wide or medium noodles

3 large carrots, scraped

3 ribs celery

1 large leek, white and light green parts only

About 2 cups chicken stock (page 157) or broth

2 tablespoons butter, margarine, or vegetable oil

2 tablespoons all-purpose flour

$^1/_4$ cup Dijon mustard, or to taste

Salt and freshly ground black pepper

Cayenne pepper

3 cups cooked chicken or turkey strips

About 1 tablespoon vegetable oil

About $^1/_2$ teaspoon sweet paprika for garnish

*F*or this casserole I have combined mustard and chicken, classic partners in the French kitchen, with carrots, leeks, celery, and noodles to make a hearty, flavorful entrée. The amount of mustard may seem surprising, but you need to be generous with it in order to season the noodles. Prepare this main course when you're looking for a great way to make use of cooked chicken or turkey, perhaps after Thanksgiving. Of course, if you don't have any leftovers, you can buy roasted chicken or turkey and cut the meat into strips.

*Makes 4 servings*

Preheat the oven to 375°F. In a large pot of boiling salted water, cook the noodles, uncovered, over high heat, stirring occasionally, until nearly tender, about 4 minutes. Drain, rinse with cold water until cool, and drain well. Transfer to a large bowl. (Add 2 to 3 tablespoons cooking water if the pasta looks sticky.)

Cut the carrots into pieces about 2 inches long. Slice the pieces lengthwise. Stack the slices and cut in thin lengthwise strips. Peel the celery with a vegetable peeler to remove the strings. Cut into thin strips about $1^1/_2$ inches long. Slit the leek twice lengthwise from the center of the white part upward. Cut the leek into pieces about $1^1/_2$ inches long. Flatten each piece and cut into thin strips. Put the strips in a bowl of cold water to rid them of any remaining sand. Lift from the bowl; the sand will sink to the bottom.

In a medium saucepan, bring 2 cups of the stock to a boil. Add the vegetables and return to a boil. Cover and cook over low heat until the vegetables are crisp-tender, about 5 minutes. Remove the vegetables with a slotted spoon to a bowl. In a measuring cup, measure the cooking liquid, adding more stock if needed to make $1^1/_2$ cups.

In a heavy, medium saucepan, melt the butter over low heat. Whisk in the flour and cook, whisking, until foaming but not browned, about 1 minute. Remove from the heat.

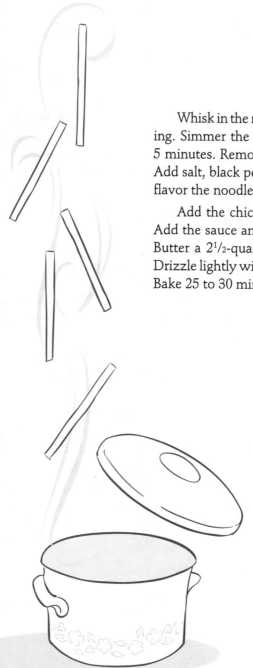

Whisk in the measured chicken stock. Bring to a boil, whisking. Simmer the sauce over low heat, whisking often, about 5 minutes. Remove from the heat and whisk in the mustard. Add salt, black pepper, and cayenne to taste. Season highly to flavor the noodles.

Add the chicken and vegetables to the noodles and mix. Add the sauce and mix well. Taste and adjust the seasonings. Butter a $2\frac{1}{2}$-quart baking dish and add the noodle mixture. Drizzle lightly with 1 tablespoon oil and sprinkle with paprika. Bake 25 to 30 minutes, or until bubbling.

# Mango Chicken with Macadamia Nuts, Orzo, and Green Onions

1 tablespoon vegetable oil

3 tablespoons minced peeled gingerroot

1¹/₃ cups orzo or riso (rice-shaped pasta), about 12 ounces

2²/₃ cups chicken stock (page 157) or broth

Salt and freshly ground black pepper

¹/₄ teaspoon hot red pepper flakes

¹/₄ cup dark raisins

3 cups diced cooked chicken

¹/₂ cup thinly sliced green onions

1¹/₂ pounds ripe mangoes, peeled and cut into ¹/₂-inch cubes (about 3 cups)

¹/₃ cup chopped toasted macadamia nuts or almonds

*The fresh flavors and bright colors make this medley of fruit, pasta, and chicken seem almost like a warm salad. Gingerroot adds a terrific taste, and orzo gives the casserole a pleasing, creamy texture. Serve this entrée with a salad of baby lettuce or with stir-fried bok choy.*

*Makes 4 to 5 servings*

Preheat the oven to 375°F. In a medium saucepan, heat the oil over medium heat. Add the gingerroot and sauté, stirring, until it softens slightly, about 30 seconds. Add the orzo and cook over low heat, stirring, 1 minute. Add the stock, salt and pepper to taste, and red pepper flakes and bring to a boil. Cover and cook over low heat 10 minutes. Scatter the raisins on top. Cook until the orzo is barely tender, about 2 more minutes. Fluff the mixture with a fork to break up any lumps. Transfer to a bowl.

Add the chicken and green onions to the orzo. Toss the mixture to combine. Add the mangoes, toss lightly, and add 2¹/₂ tablespoons of the nuts. Taste and adjust the seasonings.

Transfer the orzo mixture to a lightly oiled, shallow 3-quart casserole. Sprinkle with the remaining nuts. Bake in the center of the oven about 25 minutes, or until the top browns lightly.

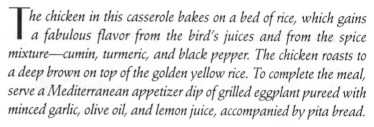

# Cumin-Scented Chicken Baked with Onion Rice

1 tablespoon vegetable oil

1 large onion, chopped

1½ cups long-grain rice

3⅓ cups cold water

¾ teaspoon salt, plus more to taste

½ teaspoon freshly ground black pepper

1 teaspoon ground cumin

½ teaspoon ground turmeric

2 pounds chicken pieces

Sweet paprika for garnish

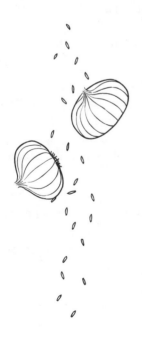

The chicken in this casserole bakes on a bed of rice, which gains a fabulous flavor from the bird's juices and from the spice mixture—cumin, turmeric, and black pepper. The chicken roasts to a deep brown on top of the golden yellow rice. To complete the meal, serve a Mediterranean appetizer dip of grilled eggplant pureed with minced garlic, olive oil, and lemon juice, accompanied by pita bread.

*Makes 4 servings*

Preheat the oven to 350°F. In a heavy, medium skillet, heat the oil over medium-high heat. Add the onion and sauté, stirring often, until golden brown, about 10 minutes.

In a shallow 3-quart baking dish, combine the onion with the rice. In a bowl, mix the water with ¾ teaspoon salt, the black pepper, cumin, and turmeric and pour it over the rice. Top with the chicken pieces and sprinkle with salt and paprika. The chicken will seem to be swimming in water, but don't worry—the water will be absorbed by the rice during baking.

Bake, uncovered, for about 1 hour 20 minutes, or until the chicken and rice are tender and the water is absorbed.

# Turkey and Corn Casserole with Olives and Raisins

3 tablespoons vegetable oil

1 large red bell pepper, diced

2 medium onions, chopped

1¼ pounds ground turkey

¼ cup chicken stock (page 157) or broth

1 teaspoon ground cumin

¼ teaspoon hot red pepper flakes

Salt and freshly ground black pepper

⅓ cup dark raisins

½ cup green olives, such as Spanish or California, pitted and diced

1 hard-boiled egg, diced

4 cups frozen corn kernels, thawed

¼ cup nonfat, low-fat, or whole milk

1 large egg

Sweet paprika for garnish

*This casserole resembles shepherd's pie, except that the delicious topping is made of pureed corn kernels instead of potato. The sweet and savory meat filling with olives and raisins is popular in many Latin American countries, but I prepare it with ground turkey instead of other meats to make it lighter. I like to add red bell peppers to the filling because of their rich, sweet taste.*

*Makes 4 servings*

Preheat the oven to 350°F. In a large nonstick skillet, heat 2 tablespoons of the oil over medium heat. Add the bell pepper and half of the chopped onions and sauté until softened, about 7 minutes. Add the turkey and sauté, stirring, until it becomes lighter, almost white, about 5 minutes. Add the stock, cumin, red pepper flakes, salt and pepper to taste, and raisins. Bring to a boil, stirring. Cook, uncovered, over medium heat 5 minutes. Remove from the heat. Stir in the olives, hard-boiled egg, and 1 cup of the corn. Taste and adjust the seasonings. Spoon the mixture into a 2-quart casserole.

In a food processor, puree the remaining 3 cups corn with the milk. In a medium skillet, heat the remaining 1 tablespoon oil over medium heat. Add the remaining chopped onions and sauté, stirring, until it begins to turn golden, about 5 minutes. Add the corn purée and cook, stirring, until the mixture is thick, about 3 minutes; watch carefully—it burns easily. Season to taste with salt and pepper.

Transfer to a bowl and let cool 10 minutes. Stir in the egg. Spoon the corn mixture over the casserole in dollops and spread gently so that the turkey mixture is completely covered. Sprinkle with paprika. Bake 40 minutes, or until the casserole is heated through and the topping sets.

# Meat Casseroles

*Beef Casserole with Sweet Potatoes and Ginger Red Wine Sauce*

*Mandarin Moussaka*

*Osso Buco and Potato Casserole with Tomato-Sage Sauce*

*Baked Beef and Green Bean Curry with Cilantro*

*Lamb and Spinach Casserole with Chickpeas and Cilantro*

*Lamb Baked with Flageolet Beans, Baby Onions, and Rosemary*

*Potato and Lecso Casserole with Salami*

During the years I spent studying cooking in Paris, I discovered how enticing beef and wine casseroles can be. The meat always turned the dry wine into a mellow, rich-tasting sauce, and the wine delicately flavored the beef.

I learned that this process is called "the flavor exchange principle"—ingredients that bake or simmer together contribute flavor to each other to achieve a new taste. For example, in Baked Beef and Green Bean Curry with Cilantro, the beef cubes give a meaty essence to the sauce and to the beans, while the curry spices and aromatic vegetables lend a lively character to the beef. A similar effect happens when you prepare the osso buco casserole, an Italian masterpiece of veal shanks in a richly flavored sauce, and Lamb Baked with Flageolet Beans, Baby Onions, and Rosemary. These casseroles make festive entrées for special-occasion meals. Because they are convenient to make ahead, they are perfect for potluck dinners.

Meat casseroles are very flexible. You can simmer many of them on top of the stove or in the oven. If the sauce is soupy, you can remove the meat and vegetables with a slotted spoon and simmer the sauce until it thickens, or you can thicken it with a slurry of cornstarch mixed with water. Remember, though, that there is nothing wrong with thin sauces. Indeed, some people prefer them, as they make a delectable moistener for an accompanying bowl of rice or couscous.

Ground meats of all types are ideal for casseroles. Combine them with vegetables and be daring with the seasonings. Many of us know shepherd's pie, made of ground beef and onions topped with mashed potatoes, but there are many other easy-to-make ground meat casseroles. Try flavoring ground beef with hoisin sauce and chile oil. Bake it with Japanese eggplant, as on page 16, for a change-of-pace entrée that's much easier to prepare than the typical Chinese stir-fry. And feel free to substitute one type of meat for another. If a recipe calls for ground lamb but your family prefers beef or veal, use them instead.

Like chicken and turkey, leftover cooked meats, whether roasted, grilled, or poached, make terrific casseroles. They can help you have dinner ready in a flash, with such entrées as Ten-Minute Beef and Bulgur Wheat Casserole with Chickpeas and Red Peppers (page 108), made with bulgur wheat, red peppers, and basil. Convenience meats, such as deli roast beef, corned beef, and sausages, are also key casserole ingredients. To prepare healthful, delicious casseroles, I use them in small amounts to flavor grains and vegetables, as in Potato and Lecso Casserole with Salami, which is generously flavored with onions and peppers.

# Beef Casserole with Sweet Potatoes and Ginger Red Wine Sauce

**1¹/₂ to 2¹/₂ tablespoons vegetable oil**

**2 pounds boneless lean beef chuck, cut into 1-inch cubes, trimmed of fat, and patted dry**

**2 medium onions, chopped**

**3 tablespoons minced peeled gingerroot**

**1 tablespoon all-purpose flour**

**³/₄ cup dry red wine**

**1¹/₄ cups water**

**2 tablespoons soy sauce**

**Freshly ground black pepper**

**1 to 1¹/₄ pounds orange-fleshed sweet potatoes or yams (about 2), peeled and cut into 1-inch cubes**

**1 pound slender carrots, scraped and cut into 1-inch pieces**

**Salt (optional)**

**1 to 2 tablespoons snipped chives for garnish (optional)**

*I*t might be surprising to add soy sauce to a red wine sauce, but this is a trick I learned in cooking school in Paris—it gives sauces for beef a deep brown color and good flavor. Fresh ginger is a great complement to the sweet vegetables and lends a pleasing accent to the red wine sauce. Serve the casserole with rice, thin rice noodles, or orzo, and green beans or a green salad.

*Makes 4 servings*

Preheat the oven to 325°F. In a heavy, large Dutch oven, heat 1¹/₂ tablespoons of the oil over medium-high heat. Add the beef in batches and brown it on all sides, 6 to 7 minutes. Using a slotted spoon, transfer the meat to a plate. Add a little more oil if the Dutch oven is dry. Add the onions to the pot and sauté over medium-low heat until they begin to brown, about 7 minutes. Add the gingerroot and sauté 30 seconds. With tongs, return the meat to the pan, reserving any juices on the plate. Sprinkle the meat with the flour, tossing lightly to coat. Cook over low heat, stirring often, 5 minutes.

Stir in the wine, water, soy sauce, and reserved meat juices. Add pepper to taste and bring to a boil, stirring often. Cover and bake 1 hour 25 minutes. Add the sweet potatoes and carrots to the casserole. Mix well to moisten with sauce. Cover and bake 45 minutes or until the beef is very tender; check with the point of a knife. Season with salt and pepper if needed. Serve the casserole sprinkled with chives if desired.

# Mandarin Moussaka

1 pound Japanese
eggplants (4 to 5)

About 3 tablespoons
vegetable oil

Salt and freshly ground
black pepper

8 ounces ground beef

3 tablespoons soy sauce

1½ cups sliced celery

1 red bell pepper, cut into
thin strips

3 tablespoons minced
peeled gingerroot

½ cup beef (page 158) or
chicken stock (page 157)
or broth

2 green onions, cut into
2-inch pieces, white
part halved lengthwise
if thick

3 tablespoons hoisin sauce
(see Note)

¼ teaspoon chile oil or hot
pepper oil (see Note)

*L*ike Greek moussaka, this casserole is composed of layers of sautéed eggplant alternating with a ground meat filling. But this casserole has new tastes and is much lighter. Instead of a cheesy topping and a tomato sauce, it boasts the pungent flavors of the Orient—fresh ginger, green onions, hoisin sauce, and chile oil. The seasonings are similar to those in braised eggplant, a popular Chinese dish, but unlike that specialty, this casserole does not require deep-frying. Serve it with plenty of steamed rice.

*Makes 3 to 4 servings*

Preheat the oven to 400°F. Cut the eggplants diagonally into slices about ⅜ inch thick. Place on a lightly oiled baking sheet and brush the eggplants lightly with about 1 tablespoon of the oil. Sprinkle with salt and pepper to taste. Bake about 10 minutes, or until just tender. Remove from the oven and set aside. Reduce the oven temperature to 350°F.

In a medium bowl, combine the beef and 1 tablespoon of the soy sauce and mix well; set aside.

In a wok or large skillet, heat 2 tablespoons of the oil over medium-high heat. Add the celery and bell pepper and sauté until crisp-tender, about 3 minutes. Remove to a bowl with a slotted spatula. Add the gingerroot to the skillet, stir, then add the beef mixture. Sauté over medium heat, stirring to break up the meat, until the beef is no longer pink, about 4 minutes.

Add the stock and remaining 2 tablespoons soy sauce to the skillet and bring to a simmer. Add the green onions, reserved celery and bell pepper, and hoisin sauce and heat 1 to 2 minutes over low heat. Remove from the heat and add the chile oil.

Lightly oil a 2-quart casserole. Layer the eggplant and meat mixture in the casserole, using 3 layers of each, beginning with the eggplant and ending with the meat. Cover and bake 30 to 40 minutes, or until the eggplant is tender and the casserole is hot and beginning to bubble.

*Note:* *Hoisin sauce, chile oil, and hot pepper oil can be found in the Asian ingredient sections of supermarkets or an Asian grocery store.*

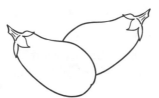

# Osso Buco and Potato Casserole with Tomato-Sage Sauce

- 2 tablespoons vegetable oil
- 1 medium onion, chopped
- 4 teaspoons all-purpose flour
- 1/3 cup dry white wine
- 1³/4 cups chicken stock (page 157), or one 14¹/2-ounce can broth
- One 14¹/2-ounce can diced tomatoes, drained
- 3 sprigs fresh thyme, or ³/4 teaspoon dried
- 1 bay leaf
- 4 veal shank slices, 1¹/2 inches thick, preferably from meaty part of hind shanks (about 2¹/2 pounds)
- Salt and freshly ground black pepper
- 2 pounds red-skinned potatoes, quartered
- 2 tablespoons chopped fresh sage

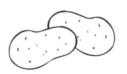

*W*hen I visit Italy, one of the specialties I enjoy most is the famous osso buco, a hearty but elegant entrée of veal shank slices in a savory sauce made from aromatic vegetables, herbs, wine, stock, and usually tomatoes. For centuries Italian cooks have been using this cut of veal to its advantage, and their method has been adopted throughout the Western world. Osso buco means "bone with a hole," which refers to the marrow bone in the center of each veal shank, and is the name of the cut of meat as well as the entrée made from it. The marrow has a luscious texture and tastes great spread on bread.

By braising the veal in a casserole in the oven, you let the meat and sauce cook evenly and don't have to worry that the flour in the sauce will stick to the bottom of the pan. During the slow cooking, the meat remains moist and becomes very tender, while the braising liquid is enriched by the natural gelatin in the bones and turns into a flavorful sauce.

Mediterranean flavors are the favorites for osso buco. In this savory version I use fresh sage and thyme. I have simplified the classic recipe by skipping the step of coating the meat with flour and browning it. This saves on fat and on dishes (and on cleaning spatters off the stove!) and is much easier to prepare. You simply put the ingredients for the braising sauce in the pan, add the veal slices, and cook the dish in the oven.

*Makes 4 servings*

Preheat the oven to 350°F. In a heavy, wide casserole or Dutch oven, heat the oil over medium heat. Add the onion and sauté until golden, about 7 minutes. Remove from the heat and stir in the flour. Return to the stove and cook over low heat, stirring, 1 minute. Remove from the heat and stir in the wine. Return to the heat and bring to a boil, stirring. Gradually stir in the stock and return to a boil, stirring. Add the tomatoes, thyme, bay leaf, and veal. Sprinkle with salt and pepper to taste. Bring to a simmer, cover, and bake 45 minutes.

Add the potatoes and 1 tablespoon of the sage to the casserole. Stir to moisten the potatoes. Cover and bake 15 minutes. Uncover and bake 1 hour, or until the veal is tender. Stir gently once or twice to moisten the potatoes. Discard the thyme sprigs and bay leaf. Stir the remaining sage into the sauce. Taste and adjust the seasonings. Serve hot.

*Note: This casserole has a fairly thin sauce. If you prefer a thicker sauce, gently remove the veal and potatoes with a slotted spoon and cover to keep them warm. Simmer the sauce over medium heat, stirring occasionally, until thickened to taste.*

# Baked Beef and Green Bean Curry with Cilantro

3 tablespoons vegetable oil

2 pounds boneless lean
  beef chuck, cut into
  1-inch cubes, trimmed
  of fat, and patted dry

1 large onion, halved and
  sliced

1 tablespoon plus
  1 teaspoon all-purpose
  flour

Two 28-ounce cans
  tomatoes, drained and
  chopped

About 1³/₄ cups water

1 tablespoon curry powder

1 teaspoon ground cumin

6 large cloves garlic,
  minced

2 jalapeño or serrano
  peppers, seeded and
  minced

2 tablespoons minced
  peeled gingerroot

Salt and freshly ground
  black pepper

¹/₃ cup minced cilantro

1 pound green beans or
  wax beans, trimmed
  and broken in half

*I*t's incredible what a difference a few spices can make! The fresh flavors of garlic, cilantro, hot peppers, and gingerroot complement the rich tomato sauce and make this casserole absolutely delicious. When yellow wax beans are available, substitute them for the green beans for a colorful variation. Serve the casserole with couscous or rice.

*Makes 4 servings*

Position a rack in the lower third of the oven and preheat to 450°F. In heavy, 4- to 5-quart, flameproof casserole or Dutch oven, heat the oil over medium-high heat. Add the beef in batches and brown on all sides, 6 to 7 minutes. Using a slotted spoon, transfer the meat to a plate.

Add the onion to the casserole and cook over low heat, stirring often, until softened, about 7 minutes. With tongs, return the meat to the pan, reserving any juices on the plate. Sprinkle the meat with the flour, tossing lightly to coat. Place in the oven and bake, uncovered, stirring once, 5 minutes. Remove the casserole and reduce the oven temperature to 325°F.

Pour the reserved juices over the beef. Stir in the tomatoes and water. Add the curry powder, cumin, garlic, jalapeños, gingerroot, salt and pepper to taste, and 2 tablespoons of the cilantro. Bring to a boil over medium-high heat, stirring often. Cover and bake, stirring and turning the beef cubes occasionally, 1 hour 15 minutes. If the casserole appears dry or the sauce is too thick, stir in another ¹/₂ cup water. Cover and bake, stirring occasionally, about 30 minutes longer, or until the beef is tender when pierced with the tip of a knife.

In a medium saucepan of boiling salted water, cook the green beans until nearly tender, about 5 minutes. Drain and rinse with cold water. Transfer the casserole to the top of the stove. Stir the beans into the casserole, pushing them down into the sauce. Simmer, uncovered, until tender, about 3 minutes. Stir in the remaining cilantro. Taste and adjust the seasonings. Serve hot.

# Lamb and Spinach Casserole with Chickpeas and Cilantro

1 to 2 tablespoons
vegetable oil

2 pounds boneless lamb
shoulder, cut into 1-inch
cubes, trimmed of fat,
and patted dry

2 large onions, halved and
sliced

6 large cloves garlic,
chopped

$^1/_3$ cup chopped cilantro

2 cups hot water

Salt and freshly ground
black pepper

2 small dried chiles, such as
*chiles japones*

Two 10-ounce packages
fresh spinach

Two 15$^1/_2$-ounce cans
chickpeas, drained

*C*ombining a generous amount of legumes with a smaller portion of meat makes good nutritional sense. This deliciously aromatic casserole illustrates how to do this and still enjoy the taste of meat. I flavor the casserole with cilantro and garlic at two different points—at the beginning so that they contribute a mellow essence to the sauce, and just before baking so that they add more of a punch. Serve this robust casserole with rice and a brightly colored vegetable, such as carrots or grilled red peppers (see page xvii).

*Makes 4 to 6 servings*

In a heavy, wide casserole or Dutch oven, heat 1 tablespoon of the oil over medium-high heat. Add the lamb in batches and brown on all sides, about 5 minutes. Using a slotted spoon, transfer the meat to a plate. Add a little more oil if the casserole is dry. Add the onions and sauté over medium heat until they begin to brown, about 7 minutes. Add half the garlic and half the cilantro and sauté 1 minute. Return the lamb and juices from the plate to the casserole and add the water, salt and pepper to taste, and dried chiles. Bring to a boil. Cover, reduce the heat, and simmer until the lamb is just tender, about 45 minutes. Discard the chiles.

Preheat the oven to 350°F. Meanwhile, in a large saucepan of boiling salted water, cook the spinach, uncovered, over high heat until just tender, about 1$^1/_2$ minutes. Drain in a colander, rinse with cold water, and drain well. Gently squeeze the spinach dry, then chop.

Skim the fat from the lamb cooking liquid. Add the chickpeas, spinach, and remaining garlic and cilantro to the casserole. Taste and adjust the seasonings. Cover and bake 30 minutes. Serve hot.

# Lamb Baked with Flageolet Beans, Baby Onions, and Rosemary

1 cup dried flageolet beans (about 7 ounces)

2 quarts plus 1 cup water

1 bay leaf

8 ounces pearl onions

2 tablespoons olive oil or vegetable oil

2 pounds boneless lamb shoulder, cut into 1-inch cubes, trimmed of fat, and patted dry

4 large cloves garlic, chopped

1 pound ripe tomatoes, peeled, seeded (see page xviii), and chopped, or one 28-ounce can tomatoes, drained and chopped

1¹/₂ tablespoons minced fresh rosemary, or 1¹/₂ teaspoons dried

¹/₂ teaspoon dried thyme

Salt and freshly ground black pepper

1 tablespoon tomato paste

2 tablespoons chopped fresh Italian parsley

4 sprigs fresh rosemary for garnish (optional)

*Flavors of the Mediterranean—rosemary, thyme, garlic, and tomatoes—accent this tasty entrée. In France, flageolet beans are the best-loved partner for lamb because they are delicate and their pale green hue makes them an attractive complement for the meat. You can usually buy them in gourmet stores, but if you can't find them, prepare this casserole with great Northern or other medium-size white beans.*

*Makes 4 servings*

Sort the beans, discarding any broken ones and any stones. In a large bowl, soak the beans in 1 quart cold water in a cool place for 8 hours or overnight. Or, for a quicker method, combine the beans and 1 quart water in a large saucepan, bring to a boil, and boil 2 minutes. Remove from the heat, cover, and let stand for 1 hour.

Rinse the beans and drain. In a medium saucepan, combine the beans with the bay leaf and 1 quart water. Bring to a boil. Cover and cook over low heat until just tender, about 1¹/₂ hours. (The beans can be kept in their cooking liquid for 1 day in the refrigerator. Reheat before continuing.) Discard the bay leaf.

In a medium saucepan, cover the pearl onions with water and bring to a boil. Cook 1 minute, rinse under cold water, drain well, and peel.

In a Dutch oven, heat the oil over medium-high heat. Add the lamb in batches and brown on all sides, about 5 minutes. Using a slotted spoon, transfer the lamb to a large bowl. Add the garlic to the Dutch oven and cook 30 seconds. Stir in the tomatoes and cook 2 minutes.

Return the lamb to the Dutch oven. Add 1 cup water, the rosemary, thyme, and a pinch of salt and pepper. Bring to a boil, cover, reduce the heat, and simmer 20 minutes. Add the pearl onions and simmer until the lamb and onions are just tender, about 25 minutes. Skim excess fat from the sauce. Stir in the tomato paste. Taste and adjust the seasonings.

Preheat the oven to 350°F. With a slotted spoon, put half of the beans in a large gratin dish or shallow baking dish in an even layer. Arrange the lamb and pearl onions in the dish. Spoon the remaining beans on top. Ladle enough of the lamb sauce into the gratin dish to moisten the beans. Cover and bake 30 minutes. Serve sprinkled with the parsley and garnished with the rosemary sprigs if desired.

# Potato and Lecso Casserole with Salami

3 tablespoons vegetable oil

2 large onions, halved and sliced thin

2 pounds green bell peppers (4 large), cut into ½-inch strips

4 teaspoons sweet paprika, plus extra for garnish

One 28-ounce can diced tomatoes, drained

Salt and freshly ground black pepper

Pinch of hot paprika or cayenne pepper (optional)

3 pounds large boiling potatoes, cooked in their skins until tender and sliced ½ inch thick

8 ounces salami, smoked sausage, or kielbasa, sliced ¼ inch thick

*S*ausages and salami are tasty flavorings for vegetables. They can play a role in nutrition-conscious eating if used in modest amounts. In this casserole, salami lends a spicy note to potatoes and lecso, *a Hungarian stew of green peppers, onions, and tomatoes seasoned with paprika. Lecso is a favorite partner for eggs and meats, and Hungarian cooks make sure to prepare a generous amount to keep on hand for casseroles and stews.*

*Serve this whole-meal casserole for a Sunday or weekday supper, accompanied by a green salad. Instead of salami, you can use kielbasa or any spicy sausage.*

*Makes 4 to 5 servings*

Preheat the oven to 350°F. To make the *lecso*, heat 2 tablespoons of the oil in a Dutch oven. Add the onions and sauté over medium-low heat until they begin to turn golden, about 10 minutes. Add the peppers and sauté, stirring occasionally, about 15 minutes. Add the sweet paprika and sauté 1 minute, stirring.

Add the tomatoes and salt and pepper to taste. Bring to a boil. Cover and simmer over low heat, stirring occasionally, about 25 minutes. Uncover and cook over medium heat, stirring often, until the mixture is thick, 5 to 10 minutes. Add the hot paprika if desired. Taste and adjust the seasonings.

Oil 2 shallow 2-quart casseroles. Spoon 1 cup *lecso* into the bottom of each casserole. In each casserole, top with a layer of potato slices, a layer of salami, another cup of *lecso*, and a final layer of potato slices.

Drizzle with the remaining tablespoon of oil and sprinkle with salt, pepper, and sweet paprika. Bake, covered, 30 minutes. Uncover and bake 15 minutes, or until the top browns lightly and the liquid begins to bubble. Heat any remaining *lecso* to serve as an accompaniment.

# Fish and Shellfish Casseroles

*Spicy Sea Bass Baked with Zucchini, Chiles, and Tomatoes*

*Fresh Salmon and Leek Casserole with Potato Topping*

*Halibut and Chickpea Casserole with Chiles, Cilantro, and Garlic*

*Cod and Bell Pepper Casserole*

*Fish and Potato Casserole with Moroccan Flavors*

*Shrimp and Mushroom Gratin with Dill-Paprika Sauce*

*Scallops and Yellow Pepper in Tarragon-Tomato Sauce*

Fish and shellfish are excellent ingredients for casseroles. These elegant seafood entrées are often my choice for entertaining. And since fish cooks rapidly, many of these casseroles have short baking times.

A practical reason to make casseroles from seafood is that you can obtain more servings of relatively expensive fish and shellfish. Casseroles are especially frugal if you combine the seafood with pasta, rice, or potatoes. To create a pleasing, nutritious dish, you can layer fish with sliced zucchini, peppers, or potatoes, as is popular in Mediterranean countries. Even beans are good with fish and shellfish, and this pairing of the humble and the luxurious has become à la mode at fine restaurants. My favorite bean partners for fish are lima beans, white beans, and chickpeas. Try, for example, the spicy and easy-to-prepare North African–style Halibut and Chickpea Casserole with Chiles, Cilantro, and Garlic for a delectable dinner entrée.

You can put raw fish in the casserole and bake it with a savory topping, such as the sautéed red and yellow peppers, thyme, and sage in Cod and Bell Pepper Casserole. This casserole is quick, easy, and light, and everyone will love the fresh flavors. For extra punch you can marinate the fish first or rub it with a spice paste.

Another technique is to partially cook the fish with seasonings before baking it. For example, in Fresh Salmon and Leek Casserole with Potato Topping, the fish is sautéed with onion and thyme and then baked under a cloud of luscious mashed potatoes.

For special occasions, you might like to bake seafood in a sauce, as in the exquisite Shrimp and Mushroom Gratin with an updated velouté sauce seasoned in the eastern European style with dill and paprika. At other times you might prefer a casserole without a sauce, to save time and calories. Most of the casseroles in this chapter do not require a sauce; it's the seafood that makes them festive.

When we think of old-fashioned fish casseroles, canned tuna and salmon come to mind. These are made less often today because fresh fish is more widely available. Still, many families have a favorite canned fish casserole that becomes a supper standard. When I was growing up, it was my mother's tuna and potato casserole. I still love it today, although I usually prepare a lighter version (page 98).

As good as fresh fish and seafood can be, I recommend keeping some frozen fish and seafood on hand for making spur-of-the-moment casseroles.

# Spicy Sea Bass Baked with Zucchini, Chiles, and Tomatoes

**1 cup fresh Italian parsley**

**1/2 small onion, quartered**

**1 tablespoon lemon juice**

**3 tablespoons olive oil**

**1 teaspoon ground cumin**

**1 teaspoon sweet paprika**

**1 1/2 pounds sea bass steaks or fillets (4 steaks or fillets), about 1 inch thick**

**Salt and freshly ground black pepper**

**8 ounces zucchini (2 small), sliced 1/2 inch thick**

**1 fresh poblano chile or small green bell pepper, cored, seeded, and cut into thin strips**

**4 large cloves garlic, minced**

**2 pounds ripe tomatoes, peeled, seeded (see page xviii), and chopped, or two 28-ounce cans tomatoes, drained and chopped**

**1 teaspoon dried thyme**

For this easy, boldly flavored casserole, the fresh fish is briefly marinated with lemon juice, cumin, and onion. Next, it bakes with its marinade in a garlic-tomato sauce flavored with a deep green poblano chile. The chile adds a touch of heat but does not impart the searing fire of jalapeño or other hot chiles. If you prefer, you can substitute a green bell pepper. Serve this appetizing entrée with rice or orzo. Instead of sea bass, you can prepare it with halibut or cod.

*Makes 4 servings*

In a food processor, chop 1/2 cup of the parsley; remove and set aside for the sauce. Put the remaining 1/2 cup parsley in the processor with the onion. Process with the pulse motion until finely chopped. Transfer to a deep dish that can hold the fish in a single layer. Add the lemon juice, 1 tablespoon of the oil, 1/2 teaspoon of the cumin, and 1/2 teaspoon of the paprika. Place the fish in the dish and coat both sides with the marinade. Sprinkle with salt and pepper to taste. Let the fish stand while you make the sauce.

In a large sauté pan, heat 1 tablespoon of the oil over medium heat, add the zucchini and salt and pepper to taste, and sauté until softened slightly, about 2 minutes. Remove to a bowl and set aside.

Preheat the oven to 375°F. Add the remaining tablespoon of oil to the pan and heat over medium heat. Add the chile and sauté 2 minutes. Add the garlic, tomatoes, remaining 1/2 teaspoon cumin, remaining 1/2 teaspoon paprika, and salt and pepper to taste and bring to a boil. Cook, stirring often, until thick, about 10 minutes. Stir in the thyme and all but 1 tablespoon of the reserved parsley. Taste and adjust the seasonings.

Put the fish and its marinade in a shallow baking dish in which it fits easily. Surround with the zucchini, and top everything with the tomato sauce. Bake, uncovered, 18 minutes, or until the fish can just be flaked and the flesh inside changes from translucent to opaque. Serve hot, sprinkled with the remaining parsley.

# Salmon and Leek Casserole
## with Potato Topping

2 pounds boiling potatoes

1/2 cup nonfat, low-fat, or whole milk

3 to 4 tablespoons butter

Salt and ground white pepper

Freshly grated nutmeg

2 tablespoons vegetable oil

1 large leek, white and light green parts, split, cleaned, and thinly sliced (about 3 cups)

1 1/2 pounds salmon fillets, skin removed, cut into 1/2-inch cubes

1 teaspoon dried thyme

Freshly ground black pepper

2 tablespoons freshly grated Parmesan cheese

*Fish baked with potatoes has become such a trendy combination in many restaurants that it might seem like a recent innovation. However, on European tables a boiled potato is the traditional partner for fish. What's different is that now the fish and potato are often baked together as one dish. Sometimes the fish is wrapped in thin slices of potato or is topped with shredded potatoes that are supposed to brown perfectly when the fish is done. Here is a much easier way to match the two—an updated fish version of a popular French bistro specialty,* hachis parmentier. *This classic dish is usually made of diced cooked meat that's covered with mashed potatoes and browned in the oven. Green beans or thin French beans (*haricots verts*) make a fitting accompaniment.*

*Makes 4 to 6 servings*

In a large saucepan of boiling salted water, cook the potatoes in their skins until tender, 30 to 35 minutes. Drain, peel, return to the saucepan, and mash. With a wooden spoon, beat in the milk and 2 to 3 tablespoons butter over low heat until the milk is absorbed and the butter melts. Season to taste with salt, white pepper, and nutmeg.

In a large, deep sauté pan, heat the oil and 1 tablespoon of the butter over medium heat. Stir in the leek, cover, and cook over medium-low heat, stirring often, until tender, about 7 minutes. Stir in the salmon and thyme. Sprinkle with salt and black pepper to taste. Cook, uncovered, over medium heat, stirring, until the outer surfaces of the salmon cubes change color to light pink, 2 to 3 minutes.

Preheat the oven to 375°F. Transfer the salmon mixture to an oiled 2-quart shallow baking dish. Gently spoon the mashed potatoes in dollops on top. Spread the potatoes lightly to completely cover the salmon mixture. Sprinkle with the cheese.

Bake 20 to 30 minutes, or until the potatoes begin to brown. Broil 1 to 2 minutes to further brown the top.

# Halibut and Chickpea Casserole with Chiles, Cilantro, and Garlic

**Two 15- or 16-ounce cans chickpeas, drained**

**4 large cloves garlic, chopped**

**2 green onions, white and green parts, chopped**

**2 tablespoons chopped cilantro or fresh Italian parsley**

**1/2 teaspoon sweet paprika**

**1/2 teaspoon dried oregano**

**Salt and freshly ground black pepper**

**1/4 cup extra virgin olive oil**

**4 small dried hot red peppers, such as *chiles japones***

**2 pounds halibut or sea bass steaks or fillets (4 steaks or fillets), about 1 inch thick**

**Cilantro or fresh Italian parsley sprigs for garnish**

*P*airing fish with chickpeas might be surprising, but it's a terrific combination that's popular in Mediterranean lands. I first tasted a fish and chickpea entrée in Florence, Italy. Flavored with olive oil and garlic, it was delectable. The pairing makes nutritional sense as well, as both fish and beans are low in fat.

When I lived in Paris in the seventies and early eighties, nouvelle cuisine *was at its height, and creative cooking was* à la mode. *Substituting fish for meat in popular entrées was one way of devising new dishes. The head chef of our cooking school, Fernand Chambrette, prepared a wonderful fish cassoulet. Instead of meat he added sautéed monkfish to the garlic- and herb-scented white bean casserole. Of course, the beans were cooked first and the fish was added toward the end so it would not overcook.*

This casserole is very easy to prepare. The bold flavors of the herbs, garlic, and hot pepper, along with fine olive oil and, of course, fresh fish, make it a memorable dish. Serve it hot or warm, accompanied by rice, crusty Italian bread, or warm pita bread.

*Makes 4 servings*

Preheat the oven to 400°F. In a medium bowl, combine the chickpeas with the garlic, green onions, cilantro, paprika, oregano, salt and pepper to taste, and 3 tablespoons of the oil. Transfer half of the mixture to a 9-inch square baking dish. Add the hot peppers and push them to the bottom of the baking dish. Set the fish on top and sprinkle with salt and pepper to taste. Top the fish with the remaining chickpea mixture. Drizzle with the remaining tablespoon of oil. Cover and bake about 30 minutes, or until the fish can just be flaked with a fork.

Discard the hot peppers or warn people not to eat them. Serve the fish garnished with cilantro or parsley sprigs.

# Cod and Bell Pepper Casserole

1/4 cup plus 1 tablespoon extra virgin olive oil

1 red bell pepper, cut into 1/2-inch squares

1 yellow bell pepper, cut into 1/2-inch squares

3 large cloves garlic, chopped

2 pounds cod or sea bass steaks or fillets (4 steaks or fillets), about 1 inch thick

1 tablespoon chopped fresh sage, or 1 teaspoon dried

1 1/2 teaspoons fresh thyme, or 1/2 teaspoon dried

1/2 teaspoon sweet paprika

Salt and freshly ground black pepper

2 tablespoons chopped fresh Italian parsley

*When I have guests for dinner, I often prepare this enticing entrée of cod or Chilean sea bass dotted with red and yellow bell peppers and fresh herbs. Use top-quality fish, fine herbs, and extra virgin olive oil and you'll have a delectable main course ready in less than half an hour. I usually serve it with basmati rice.*

*Makes 4 servings*

Preheat the oven to 400°F. In a large skillet, heat 1/4 cup of the oil over medium-low heat. Add the bell peppers and sauté until tender, about 7 minutes. Remove from the heat and stir in the garlic.

Lightly oil a baking dish large enough to hold the fish in a single layer. Set the fish in the dish and spoon the pepper mixture over. Drizzle the fish with the remaining tablespoon of oil and sprinkle with the sage, thyme, paprika, and salt and pepper to taste. Cover with foil and bake 18 to 20 minutes, or until the fish can just be flaked with a fork but is not falling apart. Taste the liquid and adjust the seasonings.

Serve the fish hot or warm, sprinkled with parsley. Spoon some of cooking juices with peppers over each piece.

# Fish and Potato Casserole with Moroccan Flavors

**8 large cloves garlic, peeled**

**¼ cup chopped cilantro, plus 1 tablespoon for garnish**

**2 teaspoons ground cumin**

**½ teaspoon crushed hot red pepper flakes**

**1 pound boiling potatoes, cooked until tender and sliced about ½ inch thick**

**Salt and freshly ground black pepper**

**2 red, green, or yellow bell peppers, cut into thin strips**

**1½ pounds ripe tomatoes, sliced ¼ inch thick**

**2 pounds fish steaks or fillets, such as halibut, cod, or sea bass (4 steaks or fillets), 1 inch thick, rinsed and patted dry**

**½ onion, thinly sliced**

**¼ cup olive oil**

T*his entrée gains its gusto from an aromatic spice paste of garlic, cilantro, cumin, and hot red pepper, which is loved in North Africa as a seasoning and marinade for fish. The spice mixture is easiest to make in a small food processor. Then it is spread on the fish, which is baked with sliced potatoes, peppers, and tomatoes. Because potatoes take longer to bake than fish, they are cooked ahead. Serve this summery casserole with a green salad or a refreshing cucumber salad.*

*Makes 4 servings*

Preheat the oven to 375°F. In a food processor, combine the garlic, ¼ cup of the cilantro, the cumin, and red pepper flakes. Process until blended into a paste.

Place the potatoes in an oiled shallow 2-quart casserole. Sprinkle with salt and pepper to taste. Top with the bell peppers. Arrange a layer of half the tomato slices over the peppers. Sprinkle with salt and pepper to taste. Top with the fish in one layer and coat evenly with the spice paste. Top with a layer of the onion slices, then the remaining tomatoes, and pour the oil over evenly.

Cover and bake 30 minutes, or until the fish can be flaked with a fork but is not falling apart. Sprinkle with the remaining 1 tablespoon cilantro and serve from the casserole.

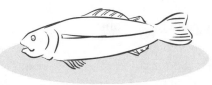

# Mushroom Gratin
## aprika Sauce

**1³/4 cups ....... .:k (page 159), or one 14¹/2-ounce can vegetable broth**

**1¹/2 pounds large shrimp, rinsed**

**2 tablespoons vegetable oil**

**1 large onion, chopped**

**8 ounces mushrooms, quartered**

**Salt and freshly ground black pepper**

**1 teaspoon sweet paprika, plus extra for garnish**

**3 tablespoons butter**

**¹/4 cup all-purpose flour**

**¹/2 cup sour cream**

**Pinch of hot paprika or cayenne pepper**

**1¹/2 teaspoons snipped fresh dill, or ¹/2 teaspoon dried**

**¹/4 cup unseasoned bread crumbs, plus more for coating**

*When I think of a classic shrimp casserole, this is what comes to mind—shrimp in a smooth, velvety sauce. But this sauce does not contain cream or egg yolks, as old-fashioned shrimp casseroles often do. Instead, the velouté sauce gains its flavor from fish or vegetable stock in which the shrimp have been cooked, thus imparting further the good taste of shrimp to the stock.*

*Makes 4 servings*

In a medium saucepan, bring the stock to a boil. Add the shrimp, stir, and return to a boil. Cover and cook over low heat 2 minutes. Set a strainer over a bowl and dump the shrimp into the strainer, reserving the stock. Rinse and shell the shrimp.

In a medium saucepan, heat 1 tablespoon of the oil over medium heat. Add the onion and sauté until softened but not browned, about 4 minutes. Add the mushrooms, salt and pepper to taste, and ¹/2 teaspoon of the paprika. Sauté 2 minutes. Remove to a strainer, reserving the liquid.

Position a rack in the upper third of the oven and preheat to 375°F. In the saucepan, melt the butter, add the flour, and whisk over low heat for 1 minute. Remove from the heat and whisk in the shrimp cooking liquid in a steady stream. Return to the heat and bring to a boil, whisking. Add the liquid from the mushroom mixture. Bring to a simmer, whisking. Cook over medium-low heat, whisking often, 7 minutes.

Spoon the sour cream into a small bowl. Whisk in ¹/2 cup of the sauce. Return the sour cream mixture to the pan of sauce. Bring to a simmer, whisking. Season with the remaining ¹/2 teaspoon paprika, a pinch of hot paprika, and the dill. Mix in the shrimp and mushrooms.

Lightly oil a shallow 2-quart baking dish and coat it with bread crumbs. Spoon the shrimp mixture into the baking dish. Sprinkle ¹/4 cup of the bread crumbs over the top. Drizzle with the remaining oil and sprinkle paprika over all. Bake 15 to 20 minutes, or until bubbling and lightly browned.

# Scallops and Yellow Pepper in Tarragon-Tomato Sauce

3 tablespoons vegetable oil, or 2 tablespoons butter and 1 tablespoon vegetable oil

1 medium onion, finely chopped

¼ cup dry white wine

1½ pounds ripe tomatoes, peeled, seeded (see page xviii), and chopped, or one 28-ounce can plus one 14-ounce can tomatoes, drained and chopped

Salt and freshly ground black pepper

Pinch of cayenne pepper

1 yellow bell pepper, cut into ½-inch squares

1½ pounds sea or bay scallops

2 tablespoons chopped fresh tarragon

The chefs at the Parisian cooking school where I studied warned the students frequently to be careful not to overcook scallops or they would be rubbery. Because scallops are delicate and cook quickly, they are best in a stovetop casserole, where you can watch them more easily than in the oven. To safeguard the scallops against overcooking, it's a good idea to cook them just before serving. If you want to get ahead, you can prepare the sauce in advance and heat it before adding the scallops and fresh tarragon. Accompany this light and elegant casserole with rice pilaf or the rice-shaped pasta known as orzo or riso.

*Makes 4 servings*

In a large skillet or sauté pan, heat 2 tablespoons of the oil over medium-low heat. Add the onion and cook, stirring, until soft but not browned, about 7 minutes. Add the wine and simmer until it evaporates, about 3 minutes.

Add the tomatoes, salt and black pepper to taste, and the cayenne and cook over medium heat, stirring often, until the mixture is thick and most of the moisture has evaporated, about 15 minutes. Taste and adjust the seasonings.

In a medium skillet, heat the remaining tablespoon of oil over medium-low heat. Add the bell pepper and sauté until just tender, about 7 minutes. Add to the tomato sauce.

Rinse the scallops and discard the small white muscle at the side of each one. Bring the sauce to a simmer and stir in 1 tablespoon of the tarragon. Add the scallops to the simmering sauce. Cook, uncovered, until the scallops are tender and turn opaque, 2 to 3 minutes. Serve sprinkled with the remaining tarragon.

# Vegetarian Main-Course Casseroles

*Potato, Pumpkin, and Chickpea Curry*

*Sweet Potatoes, Corn, and Chayote Squash in Creole Sauce*

*Cabbage and Rice Casserole with Cumin and Tomatoes*

*Pepper, Penne, and Eggplant Casserole*

*Vegetarian Paella with Artichokes, Shiitake Mushrooms, and
Red Peppers*

*Romanian Vegetable Casserole*

*Green and Red Beans with Rice*

I have always loved vegetarian menus because their use of
vegetables tends to be so much more creative than in meat-based
meals. Instead of briefly steaming and serving vegetables plain,
vegetarian cooks like to prepare them imaginatively.

With vegetables playing such a vital part in healthful eating,
most of us are making an effort to increase their proportion in our
menus. Even meat eaters are trying to include some vegetarian meals in their weekly schedules. Preparing vegetarian
casseroles is a good way to do this.

One of the best-loved bases for vegetarian casseroles is
pasta, all shapes, and not prepared just as variations of macaroni and cheese. You can bake a delectable casserole of vegetables, pasta, and tomato sauce, as in Pepper, Penne, and Eggplant
Casserole flavored with garlic and thyme.

Vegetables allied with grains also make wonderful, filling casseroles. Even the humble cabbage makes a warming, flavorful entrée when mixed with rice and bold seasonings as in Cabbage and Rice Casserole with Cumin and Tomatoes. You can keep such a casserole in the refrigerator and quickly heat it in the microwave when anyone is hungry.

Almost any cooked vegetable, whether fresh or frozen, can be tossed with cooked pasta or rice, condiments, and a bit of oil and then baked as a casserole. If you have time to add some sautéed onions, leeks, or garlic, your dish will taste even better.

The legume family gives us a great variety of nutritional powerhouses as the basis for casseroles. From dried white beans to canned chickpeas to frozen lima beans, all combine well with other vegetables. In most cases you can interchange beans according to what you have on hand. For example, Potato, Pumpkin, and Chickpea Curry is a quick and easy dish that makes use of canned chickpeas but is also delicious when made with frozen black-eyed peas or lima beans. Green and Red Beans with Rice can be made with red kidney beans, pink beans, or pinto beans.

Potatoes, sweet potatoes, corn, and winter squash also can be made into wholesome casseroles. Even children will love casseroles made with these popular vegetables.

I enjoy devising meatless versions of classics that usually contain poultry or meat, such as Vegetarian Paella with Artichokes, Shiitake Mushrooms, and Red Peppers. My students are surprised to find how well these casseroles play the role of main course, and they never miss the meat.

If you prefer, you can turn any of the casseroles in this chapter into side dishes to accompany meat, poultry, or fish. Just serve smaller portions.

# Potato, Pumpkin, and Chickpea Curry

2 tablespoons vegetable oil

1 large onion, chopped

2 large cloves garlic, chopped

1 jalapeño pepper, halved

1¼ pounds boiling potatoes

1 cup hot water

Salt and freshly ground black pepper

½ teaspoon ground turmeric

¼ teaspoon ground cumin

½ teaspoon ground allspice

Pinch of ground cloves

⅛ teaspoon ground cinnamon

1 pound winter squash (such as banana squash) or sugar pumpkin, peeled and cut into 1-inch cubes

One 8-ounce can chickpeas, drained

*I*n India, vegetable curries are made with numerous spice mixtures to give different effects, some very hot, some mild, and some sweet. In this hearty, delectable casserole, the heat of the chile is tempered by sweet spices—cinnamon, allspice, and cloves. These pumpkin pie spices also shine in vegetable casseroles containing pumpkin or winter squash.

*An easy technique for adding heat to a casserole is to use a halved jalapeño pepper. It saves time, as there's no need to chop the pepper, and people who don't enjoy fiery food can simply remove it. Serve this satisfying vegetable casserole with rice.*

### *Makes 4 servings*

Preheat the oven to 375°F. In a large skillet, heat the oil over medium heat, add the onion, and sauté until it begins to turn golden, about 7 minutes. Add the garlic and jalapeño pepper and sauté 1 minute. Transfer to a 2-quart casserole.

Peel the potatoes if desired and cut into 1-inch cubes. Add to the casserole. Add the hot water, salt and pepper to taste, and the turmeric, cumin, allspice, cloves, and cinnamon. Mix well, cover, and bake 30 minutes. Add the squash and chickpeas. Cover and bake about 45 minutes, or until the vegetables are tender.

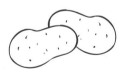

# Sweet Potatoes, Corn, and Chayote Squash in Creole Sauce

2 chayote squash (about 1 pound), see Note

1 small orange-fleshed sweet potato or yam (about 8 ounces), peeled

1 tablespoon vegetable oil

1 small onion, chopped

1/2 medium green bell pepper, cut into thin strips

1 rib celery, diced small

2 large cloves garlic, chopped

One 28-ounce can diced tomatoes, drained

1 bay leaf

1/2 teaspoon sweet paprika

Salt and freshly ground black pepper

2 teaspoons chopped fresh oregano, or 1/2 teaspoon dried

1 1/2 teaspoons fresh thyme, or 1/2 teaspoon dried

1/2 teaspoon hot pepper sauce, or more to taste

2 cups fresh or thawed frozen corn kernels

*When you combine corn and sweet potatoes in a casserole, you know everyone will love it because these vegetables are so popular. Pale green, pear-shaped chayote squashes are favorites in the South, where they are also called mirlitons. With their mild, appealing flavor, they are a perfect partner for sweet vegetables; in Puerto Rico they're even used in desserts.*

*For this colorful entrée, the vegetables are baked in a tangy tomato sauce redolent of fresh herbs and flavored with the classic Creole trio of sautéed onion, bell pepper, and celery.*

*Makes 2 to 3 servings*

Preheat the oven to 375°F. Halve the chayote squash lengthwise. In a saucepan of boiling water, simmer the chayotes, uncovered, over medium heat, for 10 minutes. Add the sweet potato and simmer 10 minutes; it should be nearly tender but not too soft. Drain and rinse the vegetables with cold water. Peel the chayote squash with a paring knife. Cut the core from the center and remove the spongy white meat around it. Cut the chayotes into 3/4-inch cubes. Cut the sweet potato into 3/4-inch cubes.

In a medium sauté pan, heat the oil over medium-low heat. Add the onion, bell pepper, and celery and cook, stirring, until the onion begins to brown, about 7 minutes. Add the garlic and cook 30 seconds. Add the tomatoes, bay leaf, paprika, and salt and pepper to taste and bring to boil. Cook, uncovered, over medium heat, stirring often, until the sauce is thick, about 10 minutes. Discard the bay leaf. Add the oregano, thyme, and hot sauce.

Add the squash, sweet potato, and corn to the sauce. Season to taste with salt and pepper. Spoon into a 2-quart casserole. Cover and bake 25 to 30 minutes, or until the vegetables are tender.

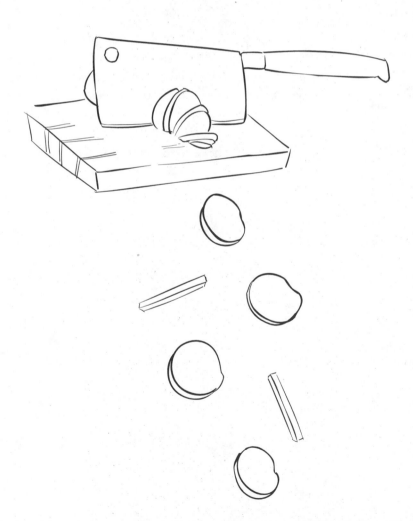

**Note:** If chayote squash is not available, substitute zucchini. Cook them whole for 10 minutes total, then cut into cubes.

# Cabbage and Rice Casserole with Cumin and Tomatoes

2 tablespoons olive oil

2 large onions, sliced

8 cups shredded cabbage (1 small head)

Salt

6 large cloves garlic, chopped

2 teaspoons ground cumin

2 cups long-grain white rice

1 quart vegetable stock (page 160) or water

$^1/_2$ teaspoon hot red pepper flakes

1 teaspoon dried oregano

One 14$^1/_2$-ounce can diced tomatoes, drained

Freshly ground black pepper

*Cabbage is one of the most healthful vegetables, and nutrition-ists encourage us to eat it often. Fresh garlic, oregano, cumin, and hot pepper flakes transform this humble vegetable into a tasty entrée and make the recommendation of eating cabbage frequently easy to follow.*

*Makes 4 servings*

Preheat the oven to 350°F. In a large casserole or Dutch oven, heat the oil over medium heat. Add the onions and sauté until softened, about 5 minutes. Add the cabbage and salt to taste, cover, and cook over low heat, stirring often, until wilted, about 5 minutes. Add the garlic, cumin, and rice and sauté about 2 minutes. Add the stock, red pepper flakes, oregano, toma-toes, and salt and black pepper to taste. Mix well and bring to a boil.

Remove from the heat, cover, and bake 30 minutes, or until the rice is tender. Taste and adjust the seasonings. Serve hot.

# Pepper, Penne, and Eggplant Casserole

**¹/₄ cup plus 1 tablespoon olive oil**

**2 green or red bell peppers, or 1 green and 1 red, cut into strips about ¹/₃ inch wide**

**1 medium eggplant (about 1¹/₄ pounds), cut into ¹/₂-inch cubes**

**Salt and freshly ground black pepper**

**4 large cloves garlic, minced**

**³/₄ to 1 pound ripe tomatoes, peeled and diced, or one 14¹/₂-ounce can diced tomatoes, drained**

**¹/₄ teaspoon hot red pepper flakes**

**1 tablespoon fresh thyme, or 1 teaspoon dried**

**8 ounces penne or penne rigate (2¹/₃ to 2¹/₂ cups)**

**¹/₄ cup plus 2 tablespoons freshly grated Parmesan cheese**

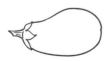

This entrée is composed mainly of summer garden vegetables—bell peppers, eggplant, and tomatoes—joined together with pasta. Flavored with garlic, thyme, and a sprinkling of Parmesan cheese, it's colorful, light, and easy to prepare. Use either the smooth type of the diagonal-cut macaroni called penne, or the ridged tubes called penne rigate. I like to serve this casserole with a diced salad of cucumbers, celery, mushrooms, tomatoes, plenty of parsley, and, when possible, a few nasturtium leaves and flowers.

*Makes 4 servings*

In a large skillet, heat 2 tablespoons of the oil over medium-high heat. Add the bell peppers and sauté 5 minutes. Add the eggplant, sprinkle with salt and pepper to taste, and sauté, stirring, 3 minutes. Cover and cook over medium heat, stirring once or twice, until the eggplant and peppers are tender, about 3 minutes. Remove from the skillet.

Preheat the oven to 375°F. Add 1 tablespoon oil to the skillet and heat over medium-low heat. Add the garlic and sauté ¹/₂ minute. Add the tomatoes, red pepper flakes, and salt and pepper to taste, and cook over medium-high heat, stirring often, until the sauce is thick, about 10 minutes. Add the thyme. Taste and adjust the seasonings.

In a large pot of boiling salted water, cook the penne until just tender, al dente, about 8 minutes. Drain, rinse, and drain well. Transfer to a large bowl. Add the tomato sauce and toss. Add the eggplant and peppers to the pasta and toss. Add 2 tablespoons Parmesan and toss again. Taste and adjust the seasonings.

Transfer the pasta mixture to an oiled 2-quart casserole. Drizzle with the remaining 2 tablespoons oil and sprinkle with the remaining ¹/₄ cup Parmesan. Bake 20 minutes, or until the top begins to brown. Serve hot.

# Vegetarian Paella with Artichokes, Shiitake Mushrooms, and Red Peppers

1 ounce dried shiitake mushrooms

Hearts of 4 large artichokes, cooked (see page xix) and quartered, or one 9-ounce package frozen artichoke hearts, or one 10-ounce can artichoke hearts, drained

3 tablespoons olive oil

1 large onion, chopped

2 large red bell peppers, cut into strips about $1/3$ inch wide

$1^1/2$ cups long-grain white rice

3 large cloves garlic, minced

$1/4$ teaspoon saffron threads

$1^1/4$ cups hot water

One $14^1/2$-ounce can vegetable broth

Salt and freshly ground black pepper

3 medium zucchini ($1/2$ to $3/4$ pound), cut into $1/2$-inch cubes

$1^1/4$ cups frozen peas, thawed

One $14^1/2$-ounce can diced tomatoes, drained

*On a vacation in Spain, my husband and I had a wonderful time driving from one town to another tasting paella. Generally it was a rich dish of rice studded with "good things," which could be seafood, chicken, or meat. Instead of the shellfish or meat, I occasionally like to perk up paella with noble vegetables—wild mushrooms, artichokes, and sweet red bell peppers. This dish has the characteristic flavor of saffron rice that makes paella so popular, but the mushrooms add a terrific new taste. Because the paella is baked briefly in a casserole, the vegetables retain their color and texture and the entrée looks beautiful.*

*With this paella as the pièce de résistance, you need only a simple salad to complete the meal. Two good choices are baby lettuces with a sherry vinegar dressing or sliced cucumbers and ripe tomatoes with a caper dressing.*

*Makes 4 to 5 servings*

In a small bowl, cover the shiitake mushrooms with hot water, pushing down any that float. Let soak 20 minutes. Remove from the water with a slotted spoon. Cut the mushrooms into bite-size pieces, discarding the stems.

If using frozen artichoke hearts, cook in boiling water in a covered pan over high heat until barely tender, about 3 minutes. Drain, rinse with cold water, drain well, and set aside.

Preheat the oven to 375°F. In a large sauté pan, heat the oil over medium heat. Add the onion and bell peppers and sauté, stirring often, until softened, about 7 minutes. Add the rice and garlic and sauté 1 minute, stirring. In a measuring cup, mix the saffron with $1^1/4$ cups hot water and add to the pan of rice. Add the broth, shiitake mushrooms, and salt and pepper to taste. Stir once and bring to a boil over high heat. Remove from the heat.

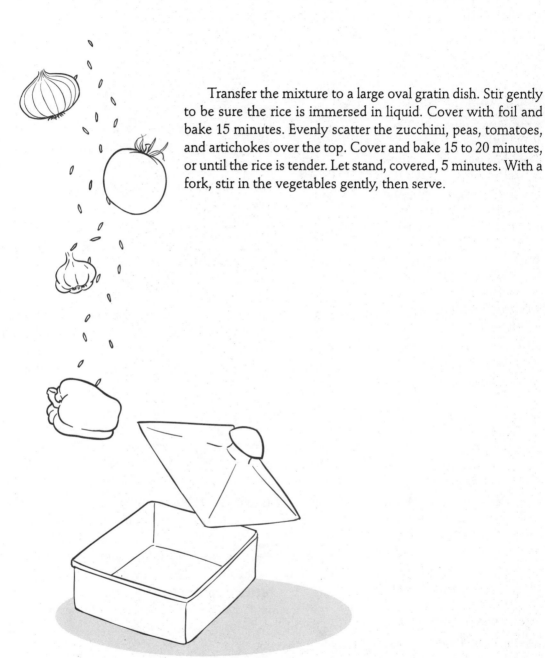

Transfer the mixture to a large oval gratin dish. Stir gently to be sure the rice is immersed in liquid. Cover with foil and bake 15 minutes. Evenly scatter the zucchini, peas, tomatoes, and artichokes over the top. Cover and bake 15 to 20 minutes, or until the rice is tender. Let stand, covered, 5 minutes. With a fork, stir in the vegetables gently, then serve.

# Romanian Vegetable Casserole

1/4 cup olive oil or
vegetable oil

3 medium onions, halved
and thinly sliced

2 red bell peppers, cut into
strips about 1/2 inch wide

1 1/2 pounds ripe tomatoes,
diced, or one 28-ounce
can diced tomatoes,
drained

4 medium boiling potatoes
(1 pound), cut into
3/4-inch cubes

Salt and freshly ground
black pepper

2 ribs celery, diced

4 ounces mushrooms, sliced

4 ounces green beans, trimmed and broken in half

2 carrots, scraped and
diced small

1 small eggplant (about
1 pound), cut into
3/4-inch cubes

2 medium zucchini (about
1/4 pound), cut into
3/4-inch cubes

3 tablespoons tomato paste

About 3/4 cup vegetable
(page 160) or chicken
stock (page 157)

4 large cloves garlic, minced

1/4 teaspoon sugar

1 teaspoon dried thyme

1/2 teaspoon dried rosemary

1/4 cup chopped fresh
Italian parsley

*V*egetable casseroles like this one, known as givetch, are popular throughout the Balkan region of Europe. Onions,
peppers, and tomatoes are sautéed, then layered with other
vegetables—potatoes, mushrooms, green beans, and carrots—and
baked until tender. Garlic and herbs lend their aroma and flavor to
the dish. Some versions include cubes of lamb, beef, or sausage,
while others are enhanced with eggs. I serve this as a vegetarian
main course accompanied by rice or pasta.

*Makes 4 servings*

Preheat the oven to 350°F. In a heavy, large skillet, heat 3 tablespoons of the oil over medium heat. Add the onions and bell
peppers and sauté until the onions brown, about 10 minutes.
Remove the onions and peppers. Add the tomatoes to the skillet and cook until thick, about 10 minutes.

Oil two 2-quart shallow baking dishes. Divide half of the
onion mixture between the dishes, top with the potatoes, and
sprinkle with salt and pepper to taste. Top with the celery,
mushrooms, green beans, and carrots and sprinkle with salt
and pepper to taste. Spoon the tomatoes and then the eggplant
on top and sprinkle with salt and pepper to taste. Top with the
zucchini and the remaining onion mixture.

In a small bowl, mix the tomato paste, remaining tablespoon oil, 1/2 cup of the stock, the garlic, sugar, thyme, rosemary, 2 tablespoons of the parsley, and salt and pepper to taste.
Pour over the vegetables. Pour the remaining stock into the
bottom of the baking dishes. Cover and bake 30 minutes; check
and add a few tablespoons stock to the bottom of the dishes if
they become dry. Cover and bake 30 more minutes or until all
the vegetables are tender. Serve hot or cold, sprinkled with the
remaining parsley.

# Green and Red Beans with Rice

2 tablespoons olive oil

2 medium onions, chopped

1 rib celery, chopped

4 large cloves garlic, chopped

$1/4$ teaspoon hot red pepper flakes

One 15-ounce can red or pinto beans, drained

1 teaspoon dried oregano

$1^1/2$ cups long-grain white rice

One $14^1/2$-ounce can chicken broth

$1^1/4$ cups hot water

1 teaspoon dried thyme

1 pound green beans, trimmed and cut into thirds

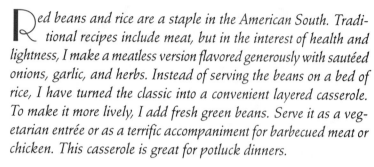

Red beans and rice are a staple in the American South. Traditional recipes include meat, but in the interest of health and lightness, I make a meatless version flavored generously with sautéed onions, garlic, and herbs. Instead of serving the beans on a bed of rice, I have turned the classic into a convenient layered casserole. To make it more lively, I add fresh green beans. Serve it as a vegetarian entrée or as a terrific accompaniment for barbecued meat or chicken. This casserole is great for potluck dinners.

*Makes 4 to 6 servings*

In a medium saucepan, heat the oil over medium heat. Add the onions and celery and sauté until the onion begins to turn golden, about 10 minutes. Add the garlic and red pepper flakes and sauté 1 minute. Transfer half of the mixture to a medium bowl and add the red beans and oregano.

Preheat the oven to 350°F. Add the rice to the mixture in the saucepan and sauté 1 minute over medium heat. Add the broth, hot water, and thyme. Bring to a boil, cover, reduce the heat to low, and cook for 12 minutes.

In another saucepan of boiling water to cover, boil the green beans, uncovered, until crisp-tender, about 5 minutes. Drain, rinse with cold water, and drain well.

Oil a $2^1/2$-quart casserole. Fluff the rice, add the green beans, and toss. Spoon 4 cups of the rice mixture into the casserole. Top with the red bean mixture, then the remaining rice. Cover and bake for 30 minutes.

# Vegetable Side-Dish Casseroles

*Broccoli and Duxelles Gratin*

*Cauliflower-Tomato Casserole with Parmesan Cheese*

*Summer Succotash*

*Potato and Leek Kugel*

*Potato and Shiitake Mushroom Gratin*

*Baked Vegetables in Ethiopian Spiced Oil*

*Zucchini-Mushroom Casserole with Pecans*

In many countries, vegetable casseroles hold a venerable place in traditional cuisine. They might be stovetop medleys that simmer over low heat, or baked mixtures of vegetables that used to be cooked in the village baker's oven. Cooks have long recognized that vegetable casseroles afford great convenience by sparing the need to prepare vegetables at the last minute.

At home today we have much more control over timing than cooks did long ago. We don't need to bake casseroles until the vegetables are mushy, which often happened when casseroles baked most of the day.

Some vegetables, such as onions, eggplant, and many root vegetables, seem made for casseroles, as the tender texture they acquire from slow baking makes them succulent. Green vegetables are less crunchy and less vivid in color in a casserole than they are when boiled just before serving.

However, they gain flavor from the sauce and the other ingredients. To maintain their texture, and shorten the baking time, many green vegetables are best precooked briefly and rinsed with cold water before being added to a casserole. Baking basically heats them within the sauce or blends the vegetables with the flavors of the seasonings.

Instead of old-fashioned casseroles made of canned vegetables and canned, thick cream soups, today most of us prefer casseroles of fresh vegetables and lighter sauces, both for their taste and for their nutritional value. Casseroles in the Mediterranean tradition, in which the vegetables are combined with tomato sauce, garlic, herbs, and a touch of olive oil, give us zesty flavors and can be low in fat.

When you want to serve a rich casserole that everyone will love, a gratin is the perfect choice. Generally a gratin is composed of a cooked vegetable with a savory sauce and a simple topping that is browned in the oven. When I studied at La Varenne Cooking School in Paris, all the students were wild about spinach gratin, with its coating of Parmesan cheese sauce accented with freshly grated nutmeg. On both sides of the Atlantic, cheese sauce and cream sauce are the time-honored choices for gratins, while the customary topping is grated Parmesan, cheddar, Swiss cheese, or bread crumbs. Sometimes I like to vary the topping by adding nuts for a crunchier result. For a leaner version, I often use tomato sauce, which also produces delicious gratins.

Gratins make menu planning easy because they can be prepared ahead and are baked and served in the same dish. There are easier versions of gratins too, made without sauces. You simply moisten the vegetable with olive oil or a little melted butter and sprinkle the gratin with the topping.

Even the most ordinary vegetable becomes elegant when transformed into a tempting gratin. All sorts of green leafy vegetables, as well as leeks, onions, and members of the squash and cabbage families, make delectable gratins. I also love gratins made of asparagus, eggplant, and mushrooms, both common and exotic. In classic cuisine, gratins are made with one vegetable, but I enjoy combining several, as in the layered Broccoli and Duxelles Gratin, in which the broccoli bakes on a bed of sautéed chopped mushrooms and is coated with a creamy sauce.

You can make irresistible casseroles from pureed vegetables. A favorite in our family is a potato kugel in which mashed potatoes are flavored with sautéed leeks or onions before being baked. For a crunchier type of kugel, use grated raw vegetables. Favorites are potatoes, carrots, and zucchini, which are mixed with eggs and seasonings before being baked.

Another satisfying type of vegetable casserole is a bread stuffing mixture enhanced with a liberal amount of vegetables, as in Zucchini-Mushroom Casserole with Pecans. This makes a great accompaniment for roast chicken and turkey, but because these types of casseroles taste so good, you'll make them whether or not you're serving roasted poultry.

# Broccoli and Duxelles Gratin

3 tablespoons butter

2 tablespoons all-purpose flour

1½ cups nonfat, low-fat, or whole milk

Salt and white pepper

Freshly grated nutmeg

¼ cup heavy cream or milk

Pinch of cayenne pepper

1½ pounds broccoli, trimmed and divided into medium-sized florets

1 tablespoon vegetable oil

2 shallots, minced

¾ pound mushrooms, finely chopped

½ cup coarsely grated Gruyère cheese

*P*repare this luxurious French-style dish for a special occasion. It's composed of a layer of broccoli resting on a bed of sautéed chopped mushrooms, topped with a creamy sauce and grated Gruyère cheese. Everyone will eat their broccoli when it's presented like this!

*Makes 4 servings*

In a heavy, medium saucepan, melt 2 tablespoons of the butter over low heat. Add the flour and cook, whisking constantly, until foaming but not browned, about 2 minutes. Remove from the heat. Gradually whisk in the milk. Bring to a boil over medium-high heat, whisking. Add salt, white pepper, and nutmeg to taste. Cook over low heat, whisking often, for 5 minutes. Whisk in the cream and bring to a boil. Cook over low heat, whisking often, until the sauce thickens, about 7 minutes. Remove from the heat and add the cayenne. Taste and adjust the seasonings.

Preheat the oven to 425°F. In a large pan of boiling salted water, cook the broccoli, uncovered, over high heat until crisp-tender, about 4 minutes. Drain in a colander, rinse with cold water until cool, and drain well.

In a large skillet, heat the oil and remaining tablespoon of butter over low heat. Add the shallots and cook, stirring, until tender, about 1½ minutes. Add the mushrooms and salt and white pepper to taste, and cook over high heat, stirring often, until most of the liquid from the mushrooms evaporates and the mixture is dry, about 8 minutes.

Spread the mushroom mixture in an even layer in a buttered, heavy 5- or 6-cup gratin dish or shallow baking dish. Top with the broccoli in a single layer. Spoon the sauce over the broccoli to coat completely. Sprinkle evenly with the cheese.

Bake 7 to 10 minutes, or until the sauce begins to bubble. Broil with the broiler door partly open just until the cheese is lightly browned, about 1 minute, turning the dish if necessary so the cheese browns evenly. Serve hot from the baking dish.

# Cauliflower-Tomato Casserole with Parmesan Cheese

1½ pounds cauliflower (1 small head), divided into medium-sized florets

1 tablespoon olive oil

1 large shallot, or 2 large cloves garlic, minced

One 28-ounce can plus one 14-ounce can diced tomatoes, drained

½ teaspoon dried thyme or oregano

Salt and freshly ground black pepper

2 tablespoons freshly grated Parmesan cheese

*Cauliflower cloaked in a chunky garlic-scented tomato sauce and topped with a light sprinkling of cheese is a tempting side dish. Fortunately, it's quick and easy to prepare. To make it even faster, you can buy ready-to-cook refrigerated or frozen cauliflower florets instead of cutting up a fresh head of cauliflower. In some markets you can also find fresh chopped garlic, another time-saver.*

*Makes 4 servings*

Preheat the oven to 425°F. In a large saucepan of boiling salted water, cook the cauliflower florets, uncovered, until just tender, about 7 minutes. Drain, rinse with cold water, and drain thoroughly.

In a large, deep skillet or sauté pan, heat the oil over medium heat. Stir in the shallot and sauté 30 seconds. Add both cans of tomatoes, thyme, and salt and pepper to taste. Cook, uncovered, over medium-high heat, stirring often, until the tomatoes are soft and the sauce is thick, about 10 minutes. Taste and adjust the seasonings.

Lightly oil a heavy 5-cup gratin dish or other shallow baking dish. Arrange the florets in a single layer in the prepared dish and spoon the sauce over. Sprinkle with the cheese. Bake 7 to 10 minutes, or until the sauce begins to bubble. If the top is not brown, broil until the cheese browns lightly, about 1 minute, checking often and turning the dish if necessary for even browning. Serve hot.

# Summer Succotash

One 10-ounce package
  frozen baby lima beans
  (about 2 cups)

1/2 pound zucchini
  (2 small), diced

1/2 pound yellow crookneck
  squash (about 2), diced

2 tablespoons vegetable oil

1 large onion, chopped

2 teaspoons sweet paprika

1 pound ripe tomatoes,
  peeled, seeded (see page
  xviii), and chopped, or
  one 28-ounce can
  tomatoes, drained and
  chopped

1 1/2 teaspoons dried
  oregano

Salt and freshly ground
  black pepper

Cayenne pepper

2 ears corn (about 1 1/4
  pounds), or 1 1/4 cups
  frozen corn kernels,
  thawed

3 tablespoons slivered
  fresh basil

*W*e tend to think of succotash as a white casserole of corn and lima beans, but it has many variations. In Latin America, for example, it is prepared as a red stew and might include winter squash in addition to beans and corn. This light and colorful succotash is inspired by that rendition and is moistened with a tomato sauce seasoned with fresh basil. Instead of winter squash, the recipe calls for green and yellow summer squashes. You can make it year-round with frozen corn, but in summer you can boost its appeal by adding fresh corn kernels.

*Makes 4 to 5 servings*

Preheat the oven to 375°F. In a medium saucepan, cook the lima beans in boiling water to cover for 3 minutes. Add the zucchini and crookneck squash and simmer until the beans and squash are nearly tender, about 2 minutes. Remove to a colander, reserving the liquid. Rinse the vegetables in the colander with cold water.

In a large sauté pan, heat the oil over medium heat. Add the onion and sauté until it begins to turn golden, about 5 minutes. Add the paprika and sauté over low heat for 1 minute, stirring. Add the tomatoes, oregano, and salt, pepper, and cayenne to taste. Stir and cook over medium heat until the sauce thickens, about 5 minutes. Remove from the heat. Add 1/3 cup cooking liquid from the beans and zucchini. Taste and adjust the seasonings. Add the corn, beans, and zucchini and mix well. Add the basil. Transfer to a 2-quart casserole. Cover and bake 20 minutes, or until the corn is tender.

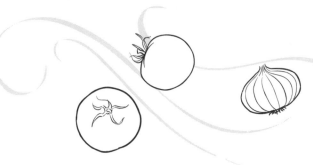

# Potato and Leek Kugel

2¹/₂ pounds large boiling potatoes, unpeeled

Salt

2 tablespoons plus 2 teaspoons vegetable oil

2 large leeks, white and light green parts, split, cleaned, and thinly sliced (4 to 4¹/₂ cups)

Freshly ground black pepper

¹/₂ cup vegetable stock (page 160)

2 large eggs

About ¹/₂ teaspoon sweet paprika

*P*otato kugel is an eastern European Jewish casserole that can be prepared with grated potatoes, but my favorite kugels are made from mashed potatoes, as in this recipe. I chose the French flavoring theme of leek and potato for this delicious kugel and seasoned it with fresh nutmeg. For a soul-satisfying dinner, I love to serve it with baked or broiled salmon and a salad of baby greens.

*Makes 6 servings*

In a large saucepan, cover the potatoes with water, add a pinch of salt, and bring to a boil. Cover and simmer over low heat until very tender, about 35 minutes. Drain, rinse briefly, and leave until cool enough to handle but still warm.

In a large sauté pan, heat 2 tablespoons of the oil. Add the leeks and salt and pepper to taste, and sauté over medium heat until softened but not browned, about 5 minutes. Cover and cook over low heat, stirring often, until tender, about 5 minutes.

Preheat the oven to 350°F. Peel the potatoes, put in a large bowl, and mash. Beat in the stock, then the eggs, just until blended. Stir in the sautéed leeks. Add ³/₄ teaspoon salt and ¹/₂ teaspoon pepper, or to taste.

Transfer the potato mixture to an oiled 8-cup casserole. Smooth the top, drizzle with the remaining 2 teaspoons oil, and sprinkle with the paprika. Bake, uncovered, about 40 minutes, or until the top is firm and light golden at the edges.

# Potato and Shiitake Mushroom Gratin

**1 ounce dried shiitake mushrooms**

**1¹/₂ pounds baking potatoes, peeled and thinly sliced**

**Salt and white pepper**

**Freshly grated nutmeg**

**3 cups whole milk**

**1 cup heavy cream**

**2 medium cloves garlic, minced**

**¹/₄ cup grated Gruyère or Swiss cheese**

Potatoes and shiitake mushrooms make terrific partners, especially in this creamy potato casserole flavored delicately with garlic and Gruyère cheese. A variation of the French classic dish *gratin dauphinois, it is greatly enhanced by the pungent taste of the mushrooms.*

*Makes 4 servings*

In a small bowl, soak the mushrooms in hot water to cover for about 20 minutes. Lift into a strainer, rinse, and drain well. Cut the mushrooms into bite-size pieces, discarding the stems.

Place the potatoes in a large bowl, season with salt, white pepper, and nutmeg to taste, and toss to distribute the seasonings.

In a heavy, medium saucepan, bring the milk to a boil, stirring occasionally. Add the potatoes and again season to taste with salt, white pepper, and nutmeg. Reduce the heat to medium and simmer, uncovered, for 10 minutes, stirring occasionally. Drain the potatoes, reserving ¹/₂ cup of the milk for the gratin; you may want to save the remaining milk for a soup.

Lightly butter a 5-cup gratin dish or other shallow baking dish. Preheat the oven to 425°F.

Return the potatoes to the saucepan and add the cream. Bring to a simmer over medium-high heat. Add the garlic. Simmer over medium heat, stirring occasionally, 10 minutes. Add the mushrooms and simmer until the potatoes are tender but not falling apart, about 5 minutes. Add the reserved ¹/₂ cup milk and return to a simmer. Taste and add more salt, white pepper, and nutmeg if needed. Spoon the mixture into the baking dish. Sprinkle with the cheese.

Bake 15 to 20 minutes, or until hot and golden brown. If the top is not golden brown, broil briefly to brown. Serve hot from the dish.

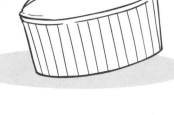

# Baked Vegetables in Ethiopian Spiced Oil

1 pound carrots, scraped
    and sliced about ¹/₂ inch
    thick

1 pound boiling potatoes,
    peeled and cut into
    1-inch cubes

Salt

1 pound cauliflower,
    divided into medium-
    sized florets

8 ounces green beans,
    trimmed and cut into
    2- to 3-inch pieces

3 tablespoons vegetable oil

1 large onion, halved and
    thinly sliced

4 cloves garlic, chopped

1 tablespoon minced
    peeled gingerroot

2 jalapeño peppers, seeded
    and chopped

1 teaspoon sweet paprika

¹/₈ to ¹/₄ teaspoon cayenne
    pepper, or to taste

¹/₄ teaspoon ground
    cinnamon

¹/₈ teaspoon ground cloves

¹/₄ teaspoon ground
    turmeric

Pinch of freshly grated
    nutmeg

Here's a great way to add pizzazz to common vegetables. Take green beans, carrots, cauliflower, or other vegetables you might have on hand and make them spicy! Jalapeño peppers and cayenne take care of that. Balance their spiciness with sautéed aromatic vegetables—onions, garlic, and gingerroot—and by the warm flavors of paprika, cinnamon, and nutmeg. Clarified butter is used for this type of casserole in Ethiopia, but I have lightened the dish by substituting a small amount of vegetable oil. These vegetables make a wonderful side dish for grilled lamb or chicken and are also a satisfying main course with rice and an accompaniment of yogurt.

*Makes 4 servings*

Preheat the oven to 350°F. In a large saucepan, combine the carrots and potatoes. Cover with water and bring to a boil. Add salt to taste and simmer, covered, until the vegetables are tender, about 10 minutes. Drain well.

In a large saucepan of boiling salted water, cook the cauliflower, uncovered, over high heat for 2 minutes. Add the green beans and cook until crisp-tender, about 2 minutes. Drain in a colander, rinse with cold water, and drain well.

In a large casserole or sauté pan, heat the oil over medium heat. Add the onion and sauté until golden brown, about 10 minutes, stirring often. Add the remaining ingredients and cook over low heat, stirring, 1 minute. Remove from the heat.

In a 2-quart casserole, mix the vegetables with the onion-spice mixture. Cover and bake 20 minutes, or until heated through. Serve hot.

# Zucchini-Mushroom Casserole with Pecans

2 tablespoons vegetable oil

12 ounces mushrooms, halved and thickly sliced

Salt and freshly ground black pepper

3 tablespoons butter or vegetable oil

2 large onions, chopped

³/₄ cup chopped celery

3 cloves garlic, chopped

¹/₂ pound zucchini (2 small), coarsely grated

¹/₂ pound day-old French or Italian bread, cut into ¹/₂-inch cubes

1 cup pecans, coarsely chopped

¹/₄ cup chopped fresh Italian parsley

1 teaspoon dried thyme

2 teaspoons chopped fresh sage, or ¹/₂ teaspoon dried

1 cup vegetable stock (page 160)

*I*n this savory casserole, the vegetables are combined with bread cubes; this is, in fact, a variation of bread stuffing. Experienced cooks know that stuffings are great accompaniments not only for roasted or grilled turkey and chicken, but for meat and fish as well. Baking stuffing in a casserole instead of inside the bird is a time-saver for a couple of reasons: an unstuffed bird roasts much faster, and spooning the mixture into a casserole is quicker than putting it inside the bird. Here's yet another advantage—you don't need to worry about fat dripping from the bird into the stuffing.

To reduce the fat in this dish, use half the amount of pecans. The casserole will still have a lively flavor from the garlic, thyme, and sage.

*Makes 6 to 8 servings*

In a large skillet, heat the oil over medium-high heat. Add the mushrooms and salt and pepper to taste and sauté until lightly browned, about 3 minutes. Transfer to a bowl.

In a skillet, melt the butter. Add the onions and celery and cook over medium-low heat, stirring, until softened, about 7 minutes. Add the garlic and cook 30 seconds. Remove from the heat.

Put the grated zucchini in a colander and squeeze out the excess liquid with your hands. Stir the zucchini into the onion mixture.

Preheat the oven to 325°F. In a large bowl, combine the bread cubes, zucchini mixture, mushrooms, pecans, parsley, thyme, sage, and a pinch of salt and pepper. Using 2 large spoons, toss until the ingredients are mixed thoroughly and the bread is moistened. Gradually add ¹/₄ cup of the stock and toss lightly. Most of the bread should be very lightly moistened; if most of it is dry, gradually add, by tablespoons, no more than ¹/₄ cup more stock. Season to taste with salt and pepper.

Transfer the stuffing to a buttered 2¹/₂-quart casserole. Cover the casserole and bake 20 minutes. Baste the stuffing by pouring ¹/₄ cup stock evenly over the top. Bake 20 more minutes and repeat with another ¹/₄ cup stock. Bake 20 minutes more; uncover for the last 10 minutes if you would like a slightly crusty top. Serve hot.

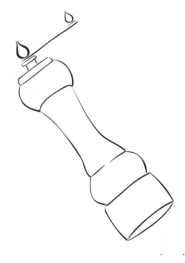

# Pasta Casseroles

*Herb Fettuccine and Garlic-Shrimp Casserole*

*Provençal Tortellini Casserole with Black Olives*

*Meaty Macaroni Casserole with Pine Nuts*

*Couscous and Turkey Casserole with Cilantro Pesto and Toasted Almonds*

*Pasta Shells Baked with Spinach and Nutmeg Cream*

*Turkey Lasagna with Sage and Fontina*

*Lemon Noodle and Crab Casserole with Curry-Ginger Sauce*

For as long as I can remember, homemade macaroni and cheese has been my favorite comfort food. Apparently many other Americans share my predilection. Americans' most popular casseroles, both for entertaining and for everyday cooking, are casseroles made of pasta. Macaroni and cheese makes a frequent appearance on many tables. When company comes, lasagna is often the preferred entrée.

This love of pasta is not surprising. Pasta is an ideal partner for just about every ingredient, from vegetables to fish to meat and, yes, to fruit. In addition, pasta casseroles suit all styles of menus. They can be as simple as spaghetti baked with tomatoes and a sprinkling of cheese. For special occasions I enjoy serving more elaborate casseroles, such as Chicken Noodle Casserole with Mustard Sauce and Vegetable Julienne (page 8).

Another reason for America's fondness for pasta casseroles is their convenience. They keep well in the refrigerator or freezer and are ready when you need them. You can heat the whole casserole in the oven or quickly warm up the number of portions you want in the microwave. As a matter of course, I add a quick-cooking vegetable, such as carrot strips or peas, to the pasta cooking liquid so that all the elements of a complete meal are in one pot.

You can enrich a pasta casserole with sauce, as in Mushroom Macaroni Pastitsio (page 83), which is topped with a cream sauce. But sauce is not absolutely necessary. Excellent casseroles can be moistened instead with a small amount of oil and sautéed or roasted vegetables, as in Double Tomato Macaroni Casserole with Peppers (page 97).

Most pasta casseroles, like Provençal Tortellini Casserole with Black Olives, make a filling meal-in-a-dish. Others, like Fusilli and Spiced Onion Casserole (page 140), can play the role of main course or hearty accompaniment.

Smaller-sized pastas are the most common for making casseroles because they are easier to mix with other ingredients. But you don't have to stick to elbow macaroni. Penne (quill-shaped pasta), shells, and spirals are also great choices. Noodles are good too, especially those that are not very long.

Occasionally I will purchase a flavored fresh pasta, such as fettuccine, rotelle, or shells seasoned with lemon, chiles, or herbs, when I want a particular taste to complement the other ingredients in the casserole. Using flavored pasta is also an easy way to give a novel twist to an old standby.

For a completely different effect, try making some of your favorite pasta casseroles using tortellini, ravioli, or other stuffed pasta shapes instead of plain pasta. When you choose a stuffed pasta with a different filling, the same recipe gains a new dimension.

# Herb Fettuccine and Garlic-Shrimp Casserole

1¼ **pounds medium or large shrimp, shelled, deveined if desired**

5 **large cloves garlic, minced**

½ **teaspoon dried thyme**

**Pinch of salt**

**Pinch of freshly ground black pepper**

¼ **cup olive oil**

⅓ **cup thinly sliced green onions, white and green parts**

8 **ounces herb-flavored fettuccine, such as basil garlic, or wide egg noodles**

1 **tablespoon chopped fresh tarragon (optional)**

2 **tablespoons butter**

*S hrimp with garlic has become an American favorite for dining out, but it deserves to be as popular in the home kitchen because it is easy to make. In this casserole I bake the garlic shrimp with fettuccine so that the delectable garlic and herb oil in which the shrimp are sautéed can permeate the pasta. A tomato salad is a pleasing complement.*

*Makes 4 servings*

In a medium bowl, combine the shrimp with the garlic, thyme, salt, pepper, and 2 tablespoons of the olive oil. Marinate at room temperature for 10 minutes.

In a heavy, large skillet, heat the remaining 2 tablespoons olive oil over medium-high heat. Add the shrimp and marinade and sauté, tossing often, 1 minute. Add the green onions and cook until the shrimp are pink, about 1 minute. Transfer the mixture to a large bowl.

Preheat the oven to 375°F. In a large pot of boiling salted water, cook the pasta over high heat, uncovered, until just tender, al dente, 2 to 5 minutes. Drain, rinse with cold water, and drain well. Transfer to the bowl of shrimp and toss to combine. Add the tarragon if desired. Taste and adjust the seasonings.

Transfer the shrimp and noodle mixture to a lightly buttered 2-quart casserole. Cut the butter into small pieces and scatter over the top. Bake, uncovered, 15 to 20 minutes, or until the casserole is heated through.

# Provençal Tortellini Casserole with Black Olives

2 tablespoons olive oil

8 ounces mushrooms, quartered

Salt and freshly ground black pepper

4 large cloves garlic, minced

2 pounds ripe tomatoes, peeled, seeded (see page xviii), and diced, or two 28-ounce cans diced tomatoes, drained

1/3 cup dry white wine

2/3 cup chicken stock (page 157) or broth

1 bay leaf

2/3 cup pitted mild black olives, such as California olives

1 1/2 teaspoons fresh thyme, or 1/2 teaspoon dried

1 tablespoon chopped fresh tarragon, or 1 teaspoon dried

3 tablespoons chopped fresh Italian parsley

Two 9-ounce packages chicken tortellini

*Inspired by the French classic* poulet à la niçoise, *in which chicken is braised with tomatoes, garlic, olives, and fresh herbs, this casserole features chicken tortellini instead of chicken pieces. It is much faster to prepare than the original—just use prepared fresh or frozen tortellini with a chicken filling. This is a lively dish to bring to potluck dinners or to fix for last-minute guests. Serve it with a green salad or a quick sauté of zucchini and yellow peppers.*

*Makes 4 to 6 servings*

In a large skillet, heat 1 tablespoon of the oil. Add the mushrooms and salt and pepper to taste, and sauté over medium-high heat until lightly browned, about 3 minutes. Remove from the skillet to a bowl. Add the remaining tablespoon of oil to the skillet. Add the garlic and cook over low heat, stirring, 30 seconds. Stir in the tomatoes, wine, stock, and bay leaf and bring to a boil. Cook, uncovered, over medium-high heat, stirring occasionally, until thick, 15 to 20 minutes. Discard the bay leaf. Add the mushrooms, olives, thyme, tarragon, and 2 tablespoons of the parsley. Taste and adjust the seasonings.

Preheat the oven to 350°F. In a large pot of boiling salted water, cook the tortellini until just tender, al dente, or according to package directions. Drain and rinse.

Spoon half the sauce into a 14 × 10-inch oval shallow casserole. Top with the pasta, then the remaining sauce. Be sure to moisten all of the pasta. Bake 15 minutes, or until the sauce just begins to bubble. Serve hot from the gratin dish. Serve sprinkled with the remaining parsley.

# Meaty Macaroni Casserole with Pine Nuts

2 tablespoons vegetable oil

1 large onion, chopped

12 ounces lean ground lamb

4 large cloves garlic, minced

1/8 teaspoon ground allspice

1/3 cup pine nuts (about 1 1/2 ounces)

1 pound ripe tomatoes, peeled, seeded (see page xviii), and chopped, or one 28-ounce can tomatoes, drained and chopped

Salt and freshly ground black pepper

2 tablespoons tomato paste

1 pound cut ziti or penne

1/4 cup freshly grated Parmesan cheese

*B* ased on a wonderful Lebanese dish, this casserole features meat with pine nuts, a favorite flavoring pair in the Middle East. Because ground lamb makes a flavorful sauce for the casserole, you can prepare the dish using a fairly small amount of meat. Serve this savory entrée with a Mediterranean chopped salad of tomatoes, cucumbers, and green onions.

*Makes 4 servings*

Preheat the oven to 350°F. In a large skillet, heat the oil over medium-low heat. Add the onion and sauté, stirring, until golden, about 7 minutes. Add the lamb, garlic, and allspice and cook over medium heat, stirring often, until the meat changes color from red to light brown, about 10 minutes. Add the pine nuts, tomatoes, and salt and pepper to taste. Cover and cook 10 minutes. Add the tomato paste and stir until blended. Cook, uncovered, until the sauce is thick, about 10 minutes. Taste and adjust the seasonings. Remove from the heat.

In a large pot of boiling salted water, cook the ziti until barely tender, al dente, about 9 minutes. Rinse with cold water and drain. Add to the pan of meat sauce and mix well. Add 2 tablespoons of the cheese and mix.

Transfer the pasta mixture to an oiled 2-quart baking dish. Sprinkle with the remaining cheese. Bake, uncovered, for 30 minutes, or until the cheese browns lightly.

# Couscous and Turkey Casserole with Cilantro Pesto and Toasted Almonds

**3¹/₂ cups chicken stock (page 157), or two 14¹/₂-ounce cans chicken broth**

**2 large carrots, scraped and sliced ¹/₂ inch thick**

**2 medium zucchini, sliced ¹/₂ inch thick**

**3 tablespoons olive oil**

**One 10-ounce package couscous (1²/₃ cups)**

**Salt and freshly ground black pepper**

**2 large cloves garlic**

**1 cup cilantro**

**¹/₂ teaspoon sweet paprika**

**Pinch of cayenne pepper**

**2 cups shredded cooked turkey or chicken**

**¹/₄ cup slivered almonds**

*Use home-cooked leftover turkey or buy cooked turkey at the deli or supermarket, and this flavorful casserole of golden couscous layered with carrots, zucchini, and turkey will be ready in minutes. The pesto is similar to the classic pesto but is flavored with cilantro instead of basil. The herb is whirled in the food processor along with garlic, then seasoned with paprika and a touch of olive oil. Since it doesn't contain cheese, it's lighter than traditional pesto.*

*Makes 4 servings*

Preheat the oven to 350°F. In a medium saucepan, bring the stock to a boil. Add the carrots, cover, and cook over low heat for 7 minutes. Add the zucchini and return to a boil. Cover and cook over low heat until the vegetables are just tender, about 5 minutes. Remove the vegetables with a slotted spoon to a bowl.

Add 1 tablespoon of the oil to the stock and return to a boil. Stir in the couscous. Cover the pan, remove from the heat, and let stand 5 minutes. Season to taste with salt and pepper.

To make the pesto, finely chop the garlic in a food processor. Add the cilantro and chop fine. Transfer to a bowl. Add the remaining 2 tablespoons oil, salt and pepper to taste, the paprika, and cayenne and mix well. Add the turkey and mix lightly. Taste and adjust the seasonings.

Spread half the couscous in an oiled 8- to 10-cup baking dish. Top with the turkey mixture, then the cooked vegetables. Top with the remaining couscous and spread it in a smooth layer. Sprinkle with the almonds. Bake, uncovered, 25 minutes, or until the almonds brown and the casserole is hot.

# Pasta Shells Baked with Spinach and Nutmeg Cream

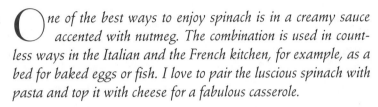

**One 10-ounce package fresh spinach**

**3 tablespoons butter or margarine**

**2 medium shallots, minced**

**$^1/_4$ cup all-purpose flour**

**$2^1/_4$ cups whole, low-fat, or nonfat milk**

**Salt and white pepper**

**Freshly grated nutmeg**

**$^1/_4$ cup heavy cream (optional)**

**3 cups medium pasta shells**

**$^1/_2$ to $^3/_4$ cup shredded Gruyère or Swiss cheese**

*O*ne of the best ways to enjoy spinach is in a creamy sauce accented with nutmeg. The combination is used in countless ways in the Italian and the French kitchen, for example, as a bed for baked eggs or fish. I love to pair the luscious spinach with pasta and top it with cheese for a fabulous casserole.

*Makes 4 to 6 servings*

In a large saucepan of boiling salted water, cook the spinach, uncovered, over high heat until wilted, about 2 minutes. Drain, rinse with cold water, and drain well. Squeeze out as much liquid as possible. Chop the spinach.

In a heavy, medium saucepan, melt the butter over low heat. Add the shallots and cook, stirring often, until soft but not brown, about 2 minutes. Remove from the heat and stir in the flour. Return to low heat and cook, stirring constantly, 1 minute. Remove from the heat. Whisk in the milk. Return to medium-high heat and cook, whisking constantly, until the sauce thickens and comes to a boil. Add salt, white pepper, and nutmeg to taste. Simmer over low heat, whisking often, 7 minutes. Add the spinach and heat through. Add the cream if desired and heat through. Taste and adjust the seasonings.

Preheat the oven to 375°F. In a large pot of boiling salted water, cook the pasta, uncovered, over high heat, stirring occasionally, until nearly tender but a little firmer than usual, about 6 minutes. Drain, rinse with cold water, and drain well. Transfer to a large bowl.

Lightly butter a 6- to 7-cup baking dish. Add the spinach sauce to the pasta and stir. Add $^1/_4$ to $^1/_2$ cup of the cheese, according to your taste. Taste the mixture and adjust the seasonings. Spoon into the baking dish. Sprinkle with the remaining $^1/_4$ cup cheese.

Bake 20 to 30 minutes, or until bubbling. Brown under the broiler, about 1 to 2 minutes. Serve from the baking dish.

# ey Lasagna with Sage and Fontina

2 tablespoons olive oil

1 medium onion, finely chopped

1/2 medium carrot, scraped and chopped

12 ounces ground turkey

2 pounds ripe tomatoes, peeled, seeded (see page xviii), and chopped, or two 28-ounce cans tomatoes, drained well

4 large cloves garlic, minced

1 bay leaf

1/2 teaspoon dried oregano

1/4 teaspoon hot red pepper flakes

Salt and freshly ground black pepper

2 tablespoons tomato paste

1 tablespoon chopped fresh sage, or 1 teaspoon dried

2 cups ricotta cheese (about 1 pound)

1 large egg

3/4 cup freshly grated Parmesan cheese

Freshly grated nutmeg

12 ounces dried lasagna noodles

2 cups shredded fontina or mozzarella cheese

*Everyone loves meaty lasagna, and there's no need to miss out on this favorite if you're trying to eat less red meat. Layer the lasagna noodles with a turkey tomato sauce flavored with oregano and fresh sage, add a ricotta layer and a topping of fontina cheese, and you'll have a lavish, festive entrée. To make the casserole leaner, you can use ground turkey breast in the sauce, substitute low-fat mozzarella cheese for the fontina, and use low-fat ricotta cheese.*

*Makes 6 to 8 servings*

In a heavy, medium casserole, heat the oil over medium heat. Add the onion and carrot and cook, stirring, until the onion is soft but not brown, about 10 minutes. Add the turkey and sauté over medium heat, crumbling with a fork, until its color lightens.

Add the tomatoes, garlic, bay leaf, oregano, red pepper flakes, and salt and pepper to taste and bring to a boil, stirring. Cover and cook over medium heat, stirring from time to time (and crushing the canned tomatoes if using), for 30 minutes. Discard the bay leaf. Stir in the tomato paste, increase the heat to medium, and simmer, uncovered, stirring often, until thick, about 10 minutes. Stir in the sage. Taste and adjust the seasonings.

For the ricotta layer, mix the ricotta, egg, and 1/2 cup of the Parmesan in a bowl. Season to taste with the nutmeg, salt, and pepper.

In a large pot of boiling salted water, cook the lasagna noodles, stirring occasionally, until flexible but not yet tender, about 7 minutes. Put in a large bowl of cold water so they don't stick to each other. Before using, put them in a single layer on towels and pat dry.

Preheat the oven to 375°F. Butter a 13 × 9-inch baking dish. Spoon 1 cup of the meat sauce on the bottom of the dish and spread evenly with a spatula. Top with a layer of lasagna noodles, cutting some noodles to fit. Sprinkle with 3/4 cup of the fontina.

Top with another layer of noodles. Top with all of the ricotta mixture by spoonfuls, carefully spreading it evenly. Top with another layer of noodles, then 1 cup of the meat sauce. Sprinkle with ³/₄ cup of the fontina.

Top with another layer of noodles. Spoon the remaining meat sauce over the noodles. Sprinkle evenly with the remaining fontina, then the remaining ¹/₄ cup Parmesan.

Bake 30 to 40 minutes, or until bubbling and lightly browned. Let stand 5 minutes so the juices are absorbed. Cut into squares and serve.

# Lemon Noodle and Crab Casserole with Curry-Ginger Sauce

- 3 tablespoons vegetable oil
- 1 medium onion, chopped
- 1 tablespoon minced peeled gingerroot
- 2 large cloves garlic, minced
- 2 teaspoons ground cumin
- 2 teaspoons ground coriander
- 1/2 teaspoon ground turmeric
- 1/8 teaspoon cayenne pepper
- 1 pound ripe tomatoes, peeled, seeded (see page xviii), and coarsely chopped, or one 28-ounce can tomatoes, drained and chopped
- 1 teaspoon finely grated lemon zest
- 3/4 pound crabmeat, picked over, any shell and cartilage discarded, meat chopped
- 8 ounces lemon-flavored noodles or egg noodles
- Salt and freshly ground black pepper
- 1 tablespoon chopped cilantro or fresh Italian parsley for garnish
- Lemon wedges for serving

*C*oriander, cumin, and ginger add spice to the sauce, but don't make the casserole so hot that it overpowers the crab's delicate taste. I like to add a touch of grated lemon rind and use lemon-flavored pasta in the casserole, because the citrus flavor complements the rich crabmeat. If real crabmeat is not available, you can use imitation crab, or surimi. For such a good-tasting entrée, this casserole is surprisingly quick and easy to prepare.

*Makes 4 servings*

In a medium sauté pan, heat the oil over medium-low heat. Add the onion and cook until softened, about 7 minutes. Add the gingerroot, garlic, cumin, coriander, turmeric, and cayenne and cook, stirring, 1 minute. Add the tomatoes and cook over medium heat, stirring often, until the sauce is thick, 10 to 15 minutes. Stir in the lemon zest and crabmeat.

Preheat the oven to 375°F. In a large pot of boiling salted water, cook the noodles until barely tender, al dente, 2 to 5 minutes. Drain, rinse with cold water, and drain well. Transfer to a bowl and toss with the crab sauce. Season to taste with salt and pepper.

Transfer the noodle mixture to a lightly oiled 2-quart casserole. Cover and bake 20 minutes, or until heated through. Serve sprinkled with cilantro or parsley. Accompany with lemon wedges.

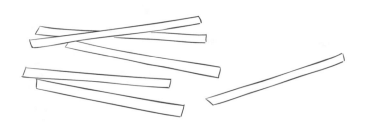

# Casseroles of Rice and Other Grains

*Rice and Pepper Casserole with Basil and Parmesan*

*Rice Pilaf with Dried Cranberries and Pecans*

*Rice Baked with Eggplant and Pine Nuts*

*Vegetable Biriani with Saffron, Ginger, and Garlic*

*Spicy Bulgur Wheat and Smoked Turkey Casserole with Tomatoes and Mint*

*Brown Rice with Roquefort and Onions*

*Barley and Vegetable Casserole with Yogurt-Chive Topping*

*Buckwheat, Noodle, and Cottage Cheese Casserole with Dill*

Like pasta, rice and most grains have a neutral flavor that enables them to marry well with practically every ingredient and every seasoning. Centuries ago cooks learned that rice makes excellent casseroles, whether combined with chicken, seafood, meat, or vegetables. Spaniards are proud of their paella, with richly flavored, golden grains of rice dotted with chicken, seafood, and tomato, and redolent of saffron and garlic. Closely related is *arroz con pollo,* made in both Spain and Latin America, in which chicken and rice cook with peppers and cumin. A hotter cousin is the Louisiana specialty jambalaya, which includes shellfish, chicken, or spicy sausage as well as aromatic vegetables and plenty of hot pepper. In India a favorite dish is *biriani,* a casserole of marinated lamb or chicken seasoned with coriander, cumin, cardamom, and other spices, cooked with onions and garlic, and layered with rice.

All these dishes benefit from the flavor that the meat, seafood, or vegetables impart to the rice. In their classic forms, they are fairly involved but can be used as inspiration for easier, lighter, modern casseroles, such as Vegetarian Paella with Artichokes, Shiitake Mushrooms, and Red Peppers (page 42).

You can choose among several techniques for preparing rice for a casserole: put raw rice in the casserole so that it cooks in the oven along with the liquid and seasonings, as in Rice Pilaf with Dried Cranberries and Pecans; use partially cooked rice, which finishes cooking in the oven, as in Green and Red Beans with Rice (page 45); or use cooked rice, which needs only to heat through with the other ingredients, as in Shrimp, Rice, and Tomatoes Baked with Capers (page 135).

Which method to choose is often a matter of convenience. If you have cooked rice on hand in the refrigerator or freezer, use it in a casserole instead of starting with raw rice. Use partly or fully cooked rice when you're combining it with other cooked ingredients.

Long- or short-grain rice can be used for casseroles. Fragrant basmati rice is preferred in certain lavish Indian casseroles, but it must be handled gently so that its long, delicate grains are not crushed.

Nutritious brown rice provides tasty variations for your rice casseroles. Since brown rice takes about 45 minutes to cook, it's a good idea to cook enough for several meals so you'll have some on hand for casseroles. When time is short, you can make casseroles using quick-cooking or "instant" brown rice, which is ready in 10 minutes and is widely available at supermarkets.

The noble member of this group is wild rice, which is wonderful in casseroles with poultry, fish, and vegetables. For special occasions, combine it with other luxurious ingredients, as in Wild Rice and Shrimp Casserole with Asparagus and Shallots (page 84).

Bulgur wheat, a favorite grain in Middle Eastern cooking, is easy to use in casseroles. One of the most ancient forms of fast food, bulgur wheat cooks in 15 minutes. It is made of wheat that has been cracked and steamed, and its nutty taste makes it a perfect partner for vegetables, chicken, and turkey. It's also great for quick stovetop casseroles.

Pearl barley is a popular grain for soups, and its creamy texture makes it an appealing casserole ingredient as well. At natural foods stores you can find a fast-cooking form of barley, which takes only 10 minutes to cook instead of the usual 40 minutes.

Buckwheat kernels, or kasha, also cook quickly. Strictly speaking, buckwheat is not a grain, yet from a culinary standpoint, it's treated as one. Unlike other grains, it has a bold flavor and is good combined with mild foods like pasta and eggs.

Corn is another grain that is sensational in casseroles, whether fresh, frozen, or canned. You can also use corn in its dry forms, fine or coarse cornmeal, by cooking them as cornmeal mush, also known as polenta, and layering the mixture with vegetables, cheeses, and tomato sauce.

In addition to these common varieties, you can make casseroles from more exotic grains, such as wheat berries, quinoa, millet, and amaranth. You can find them at natural foods stores and some supermarkets. Cook them according to the package instructions and substitute them for cooked rice in your favorite entrées to give them a new twist.

For the health-conscious cook, grains are ideal casserole ingredients. They don't even need to be mixed with a sauce. A little oil or sautéed vegetables along with chicken or vegetable stock are all that are needed to make sure the casserole is moist, flavorful, and low in fat. For a richer entrée, you can mix in a little sour cream, cottage cheese, or both, as in Buckwheat, Noodle, and Cottage Cheese Casserole with Dill. If you want a creamy taste without the fat, simply substitute low-fat or nonfat versions of these dairy products.

# Rice and Pepper Casserole with Basil and Parmesan

**2 to 3 tablespoons olive oil or vegetable oil**

**1 medium onion, finely chopped**

**1 red bell pepper, diced small**

**1 yellow bell pepper, diced small**

**1¹/₂ cups long-grain white rice**

**3 cups boiling water**

**Salt and freshly ground black pepper**

**¹/₄ cup shredded fresh basil**

**¹/₂ cup freshly grated Parmesan cheese**

Red and yellow peppers and green basil give this casserole color and charm. The cheese makes it a richly flavored dish, suitable as a main course when joined with stewed vegetables. It can also be served as a tasty accompaniment for simply prepared meat or poultry, such as grilled steak or sautéed turkey cutlets.

*Makes 4 to 6 servings*

Preheat the oven to 350°F. Oil a 2-quart casserole. In a large sauté pan or skillet, heat the oil over medium-low heat. Add the onion and bell peppers and cook, stirring often, until soft but not brown, about 7 minutes. Add the rice and sauté, stirring, until the grains turn milky white, about 2 minutes. Transfer the mixture to the casserole.

Pour the boiling water over the rice mixture. Add a pinch of salt and pepper. Cover tightly and bake for 30 minutes, or until the rice is just tender.

With a fork, fluff the rice and gently stir in the basil and ¹/₄ cup of the Parmesan. Taste and adjust the seasonings. Sprinkle with the remaining ¹/₄ cup cheese. Bake, uncovered, 10 minutes, or until the cheese melts and browns lightly. If the cheese does not brown, broil about 1 minute to brown.

# Rice Pilaf with Dried Cranberries and Pecans

2 tablespoons butter or
   vegetable oil

1 medium onion,
   finely chopped

1 cup long-grain white rice

2 cups boiling water

1/3 cup dried cranberries

1/2 teaspoon salt

Pinch of freshly ground
   black pepper

1/2 cup pecan halves

2 tablespoons chopped
   fresh Italian parsley

Pecans and dried cranberries lend an American touch to this Middle Eastern pilaf, usually made with almonds and raisins. This casserole is a perfect accompaniment for grilled lamb chops, roast leg of lamb, or grilled or roasted chicken or duck. It's also terrific with the Thanksgiving turkey.

*Makes 4 servings*

Preheat the oven to 350°F. In a wide, ovenproof saucepan or sauté pan, melt the butter over low heat. Add the onion and cook, stirring often, until soft but not brown, about 5 minutes. Add the rice and cook, stirring, until the grains turn milky white, about 2 minutes. Add the boiling water, cranberries, salt, and pepper and bring to a boil.

Cover with a round of buttered parchment paper or foil and top with a lid. Bake for 20 minutes. Taste; if the rice is not yet tender, bake 2 more minutes. Remove from the oven and let the rice stand, covered, for 10 minutes.

While the rice is standing, toast the pecans on a baking sheet in the oven for about 5 minutes, or until aromatic. Using a fork, gently stir the pecans and parsley into the rice. Taste and adjust the seasonings. Serve hot.

# Rice Baked with Eggplant and Pine Nuts

**¹/₄ cup pine nuts**

**2 sprigs fresh thyme, or ¹/₂ teaspoon dried**

**1 bay leaf**

**¹/₄ cup olive oil or vegetable oil**

**2 medium onions, chopped**

**2 large cloves garlic, minced**

**1¹/₂ cups long-grain white rice**

**3 cups vegetable (page 160) or chicken stock (page 157) or broth**

**Salt and freshly ground black pepper**

**6 Japanese eggplants, or 2 medium Italian eggplants (peeled if skins are tough), cut into small cubes**

**¹/₄ cup chopped fresh Italian parsley**

*L*ike mushrooms, eggplant has a meaty texture and marries well with rice to make vegetarian main courses. In this one, the flavorings are simple—sautéed onions, garlic, and thyme; it's the toasted pine nuts that lend a festive accent. Serve this casserole with a colorful accompaniment, such as a tomato salad with basil or a sauté of mixed bell peppers. If you like, pass a bowl of grated Parmesan cheese for sprinkling lightly on each portion.

*Makes 6 servings*

Preheat the oven to 350°F. On a baking sheet, toast the pine nuts in the oven about 5 minutes, or until light golden. Transfer to a plate.

Wrap the thyme sprigs and bay leaf in a piece of cheesecloth and tie tightly. (If using dried thyme, skip this step.) In a medium ovenproof sauté pan, heat 2 tablespoons of the oil over medium-low heat. Add the onions and cook, stirring often, until soft but not brown, about 7 minutes. Add the garlic and sauté 30 seconds. Add the rice and sauté, stirring, until the grains begin to turn milky white, about 2 minutes.

In a medium saucepan, bring the stock to a boil over high heat. Pour it over the rice and stir once. Add the herbs in cheesecloth (or just the bay leaf if using dried thyme, which is added later) and submerge in the liquid. Add a pinch of salt and pepper. Raise the heat to high and bring the mixture to a boil. Cover tightly and bake about 20 minutes, or until the rice is just tender.

In a Dutch oven, heat the remaining 2 tablespoons oil over medium heat. Add the eggplant cubes, sprinkle lightly with salt and pepper, and sauté until the pan looks dry, about 3 minutes. Cover and cook over medium-low heat, stirring often, until the eggplant is tender, about 10 minutes.

Discard the herb bag (or bay leaf) from the rice. If using dried thyme, sprinkle over the rice. Using a fork, fluff the rice and gently stir in the toasted pine nuts, 3 tablespoons of the parsley, and the eggplant. Taste and adjust the seasonings. Cover, return to the oven, and bake 10 minutes to heat through. Serve hot, sprinkled with the remaining parsley.

# Vegetable Biriani with Saffron, Ginger, and Garlic

2 to 3 tablespoons butter
   or vegetable oil

1 medium onion,
   finely chopped

1 tablespoon minced
   peeled gingerroot

3 large cloves garlic,
   chopped

1¼ cups basmati rice,
   rinsed and drained

2 cups water

¼ teaspoon saffron threads

½ teaspoon salt

Pinch of freshly ground
   black pepper

½ teaspoon ground
   coriander

1 bay leaf

1 cinnamon stick

5 cardamom pods
   (optional), see Note

3 tablespoons chopped
   cilantro

2 cups small cauliflower
   florets, cooked and
   drained

1 cup fresh or frozen peas,
   cooked and drained

¼ cup toasted cashews or
   almonds for garnish
   (optional)

In traditional Indian cooking, biriani is a festive rice casserole reserved for weddings, festivals, or banquets. Usually it's made of marinated chicken or lamb seasoned with a variety of spices, cooked with onions and garlic, and layered with fragrant basmati rice. For an extra festive touch, biriani is sometimes garnished with toasted nuts. Today some Indian restaurants offer vegetarian versions. At an Indian restaurant in Santa Monica, California, I particularly enjoyed a vegetable biriani that was flavored with cilantro leaves. This is an easy adaptation of that dish. If you don't have basmati rice, you can use long-grain white rice.

*Makes 4 servings*

Preheat the oven to 350°F. In a wide saucepan or sauté pan, melt the butter over low heat. Add the onion and cook, stirring often, until soft but not brown, about 5 minutes. Add the gingerroot and garlic and cook, stirring, 1 minute. Add the rice, water, saffron, salt, pepper, coriander, bay leaf, cinnamon stick, and cardamom pods. Bring to a boil. Cover and cook over low heat until the rice is barely tender, about 15 minutes. Discard the bay leaf. With a fork, lightly fluff the rice and stir in 2 tablespoons of the cilantro.

Transfer half the rice to a greased 2-quart casserole. Top with the cauliflower and peas. Sprinkle the vegetables lightly with salt and pepper. Top with the remaining rice. Cover and bake 15 minutes. Serve sprinkled with the remaining cilantro and with nuts if desired.

*Note: Cardamom pods can be found in some supermarkets and Middle Eastern groceries.*

# Spicy Bulgur Wheat and Smoked Turkey Casserole with Tomatoes and Mint

1 cup bulgur wheat

2 cups boiling water

3 tablespoons olive oil

1 medium onion, chopped

1 red bell pepper, diced

1 green bell pepper, diced

2 cups thin strips smoked turkey

1 tablespoon tomato paste

1 tablespoon fresh lemon juice, or more to taste

Salt and freshly ground black pepper

Cayenne pepper

²/₃ cup chopped fresh Italian parsley, plus extra for garnish

³/₄ cup chopped fresh mint, plus extra for garnish

3 green onions, cut into thin slices, plus extra for garnish

3 plum tomatoes, sliced

Lemon wedges for serving

Bulgur wheat is best known as a major ingredient of tabbouleh, an internationally fashionable Lebanese salad flavored with plenty of parsley, fresh mint, green onions, and tomatoes. These ingredients appear in this casserole, too. To accentuate its freshness, garnish this entrée with lemon wedges, chopped green onions, and mint.

*Makes 5 to 6 servings*

Preheat the oven to 350°F. In a medium saucepan, combine the bulgur wheat and boiling water. Cover and cook over low heat 10 minutes.

In a large skillet, heat 2 tablespoons of the oil over medium heat. Add the chopped onion and bell peppers and sauté, stirring often, until nearly tender but not brown, about 7 minutes. Remove from the heat and stir in the turkey. Add the bulgur wheat and mix lightly.

In a small bowl, mix the tomato paste with the remaining tablespoon oil, the lemon juice, and salt, pepper, and cayenne to taste. Add to the bulgur wheat. Lightly mix in the parsley, mint, and green onions. Taste and adjust the seasonings. Transfer to an oiled 2-quart casserole. Top with the sliced tomatoes in a single layer.

Cover and bake 15 minutes to heat through. Serve sprinkled with chopped parsley, mint, and green onions. Serve with lemon wedges.

# Brown Rice with Roquefort and Onions

5 stems parsley (without leaves)

1 fresh sprig thyme, or ¼ teaspoon dried

1 bay leaf

2 cups hot chicken stock (page 157), vegetable stock (page 160), or water

3 to 4 tablespoons unsalted butter or vegetable oil

2 large onions, chopped

1 cup long-grain brown rice

¼ teaspoon salt

Freshly ground black pepper

⅓ cup crumbled Roquefort cheese

1 tablespoon chopped fresh Italian parsley (optional)

The inspiration for this entrée was a quiche of Roquefort cheese and onions that I enjoyed at Androuet, the famous Parisian restaurant specializing in cheese. This casserole is much easier to make than a quiche and much more reasonable from a nutritional viewpoint because it does not contain cream and eggs. It still is rich in taste, and the combination of the flavors is outstanding.

*Makes 4 servings*

Preheat the oven to 350°F. Place the parsley stems, thyme, and bay leaf on a piece of cheesecloth, fold to enclose, and tie tightly. Butter a round of parchment paper the diameter of the pan to be used for cooking the rice (medium sauté pan or skillet). In a small saucepan, heat the stock to a simmer. Cover and keep warm.

In a medium ovenproof sauté pan, heat 2 to 3 tablespoons of the butter over low heat. Add the onions and cook over medium-low heat, stirring often, until the pan is dry, about 5 minutes. Cover and cook over low heat, stirring often, until very tender, about 10 minutes. Remove the onions to a bowl.

In the sauté pan, heat the remaining tablespoon butter. Add the rice and sauté over medium heat, stirring, about 3 minutes.

Pour the hot stock over the rice and stir once. Add the cheesecloth bag and submerge it in the liquid. Add the salt and pepper and bring the mixture to a boil. Press the round of buttered paper, buttered side down, onto the rice, and cover the pan with a tight lid. Bake, without stirring, 35 minutes. Taste the rice; if it is too chewy or if the liquid is not absorbed, bake 2 more minutes. Discard the cheesecloth bag. Scatter the sautéed onions and Roquefort over the rice and cover.

Let the rice stand about 10 minutes and then fluff with a fork. Continue tossing with a fork until the onions and Roquefort are thoroughly mixed into the rice. Taste and adjust the seasonings. Transfer the rice to a serving dish. Serve sprinkled with parsley if desired.

# Barley and Vegetable Casserole with Yogurt-Chive Topping

3 tablespoons vegetable oil
   or butter

3 large onions, sliced

Salt and freshly ground
   black pepper

8 ounces mushrooms, sliced

1 teaspoon dried thyme

1 cup medium pearl barley

3 large carrots, scraped
   and diced

$1/3$ cup chopped fresh
   Italian parsley

3 cups vegetable (page 160)
   or chicken stock (page
   157)

## Topping (optional)

1 cup plain nonfat, low-fat,
   or whole yogurt

Salt to taste

Cayenne pepper

1 tablespoon snipped chives

*B*arley isn't just for soup. It makes wonderful, hearty casseroles like this one, in which onion compote lends a sweet and savory accent. Serve it as a vegetarian main course or as a tasty side dish with chicken or steak; in the latter case you won't need the topping.

*Makes 4 to 6 servings*

In a heavy Dutch oven, heat the oil over low heat. Add the onions, a pinch of salt, and pepper to taste. Cover and cook, stirring often, until tender, about 20 minutes. Uncover and cook 5 minutes longer. Add the mushrooms and thyme and sauté over medium heat, stirring often, until slightly softened, about 3 minutes. Stir in the barley and sauté 1 minute. Remove from the heat. Stir in the carrots and parsley. Preheat the oven to 350°F. Transfer the mixture to an oiled 2-quart casserole.

In a small saucepan, bring the stock to a boil, then pour over the barley mixture. Cover and bake, stirring 3 or 4 times, about $1^{1/4}$ hours, or until the barley is tender. Fluff with a fork before serving.

If using the topping, in a small bowl, mix the yogurt, salt and cayenne to taste, and chives. Serve each portion with the yogurt-chive topping.

# Buckwheat, Noodle, and Cottage Cheese Casserole with Dill

7 to 8 ounces medium egg noodles

1/4 cup vegetable oil or butter

2 large onions, halved and sliced

3 large eggs

1 cup medium or large kasha (roasted buckwheat groats or kernels)

Salt and freshly ground black pepper

2 cups hot vegetable stock (page 160) or water

1 cup creamed, low-fat, or nonfat cottage cheese

1/2 cup regular, low-fat, or nonfat sour cream

1/4 cup snipped fresh dill, or 1 tablespoon dried

Sweet paprika for garnish

*K*asha, or roasted buckwheat, which is popular in Russia, gives this entrée its character. The assertive flavor of buckwheat makes it a perfect partner for bland ingredients like noodles, cottage cheese, and sour cream. Fresh dill adds a lively touch. Serve a red cabbage salad with cucumbers as a colorful accompaniment.

*Makes 4 to 5 main-course servings;
6 to 8 side-dish servings*

Preheat the oven to 350°F. In a large pot of boiling salted water, cook the noodles, uncovered, over high heat until nearly tender but firmer than usual, about 4 minutes. Drain, rinse thoroughly with cold water, and drain well. Transfer to a large bowl.

In a heavy, large skillet, heat 3 tablespoons of the oil over medium-low heat. Add the onions and cook, stirring often, until brown, about 15 minutes; cover the onions if they turn too dark. Transfer to a bowl; cover to keep warm.

In a wide bowl, beat 1 egg. Add the kasha and stir with a fork until the grains are thoroughly coated. Put the mixture in a heavy skillet and sauté over medium heat until dry, about 3 minutes, stirring to keep the grains separate. Add salt and pepper to taste and the hot stock and stir. Cover and cook over low heat until all the stock is absorbed, about 15 minutes. Fluff with a fork.

In a small bowl, beat the remaining eggs and add to the noodles. Add the cottage cheese, sour cream, and dill and mix well. Stir in the onions and kasha. Taste and adjust the seasonings; the mixture should be seasoned generously. Transfer the mixture to a buttered or oiled 2-quart baking dish. Drizzle with the remaining tablespoon oil or dot with butter, then dust with paprika. Bake, uncovered, 1 hour, or until set. Serve from the baking dish.

# Casseroles for Company

*Mushroom Macaroni Pastitsio*

*Wild Rice and Shrimp Casserole with Asparagus and Shallots*

*Orange Chicken and Pasta Casserole with Soy Sauce and Ginger*

*Chicken and Shiitake Mushroom Cassoulet*

*Seafood Terrine with Tomato-Tarragon Sauce*

*Zucchini Gratin with Potatoes, Tomatoes, and Parmesan*

*Salmon and Rice Baked with Garlic and Saffron*

Throughout history, many grand casseroles undoubtedly were developed for get-togethers with family and friends. Such lavish dishes as jambalaya, paella, and cassoulet contain a rather long list of ingredients and are made in generous quantities. Thus, they are not for everyday meals; they're for celebrating.

But casseroles for dinner parties aren't necessarily more complicated than others. They are simply casseroles for which you take a little more care in preparing than dishes for everyday meals. I find casseroles to be perfect for entertaining because I can make them ahead and have more time to spend with my guests instead of preparing last-minute dishes in the kitchen.

When guests are coming for dinner, you will probably want to feature special ingredients such as salmon, shrimp, exotic mushrooms, or wild rice in your casseroles or use ordinary foods in a festive way. If you're serving chicken, try marinating it to add extra flavor, as in Orange Chicken Pasta Casserole with Soy Sauce and Ginger. Instead of using canned beans, use cooked dried beans for a more delicate taste, as in Chicken and Shiitake Mushroom Cassoulet, a new twist on a traditional favorite.

Depending on your company, you might like to opt for familiar tastes that everyone will love. This is especially true if some of the guests are children, who will enjoy casseroles of pasta, such as Mushroom Macaroni Pastitsio, with its pizzalike seasoning and cheese topping. Casseroles containing corn or potatoes will also be popular with all members of the family.

In fact, most of the casseroles in this book can appear in your menus for entertaining. Even the quickest, easiest ones are fine for a casual get-together. With today's busy lifestyles, everyone appreciates home cooking, even in a simple country style.

Part of making a casserole festive is presentation. An easy way to add a lively touch is to set a few sprigs of fresh herbs next to each portion, such as a basil sprig with the cassoulet. Of course, have the garnish complement the flavors of the casserole. Lemon, lime, or orange slices or wedges also add color and flavor; a few lemon slices, for example, look nice next to Salmon and Rice Baked with Garlic and Saffron.

Casseroles are perfect for holiday meals. In many families they are a staple on the holiday dinner table. Whether your guests prefer meat, fish, or vegetarian dishes, there's a tasty casserole that's sure to please them.

# Mushroom Macaroni Pastitsio

**2 tablespoons vegetable oil or soft butter**

**1 small onion, chopped**

**12 ounces mushrooms, diced or coarsely chopped**

**¹/₄ cup dry white wine**

**One 14¹/₂-ounce can diced tomatoes, drained**

**Salt and freshly ground black pepper**

**¹/₂ teaspoon dried oregano**

**Pinch of ground cinnamon**

**8 ounces large elbow macaroni**

**¹/₄ cup plus 2 tablespoons freshly grated Parmesan cheese**

**1¹/₂ tablespoons butter**

**2 tablespoons all-purpose flour**

**1¹/₂ cups nonfat, low-fat, or whole milk**

**Freshly grated nutmeg**

**3 tablespoons bread crumbs**

*A*lthough traditional versions of the Greek pasta casserole known as pastitsio *often are made with meat, I like to substitute mushrooms. This recipe is a lightened version of the classic but is still luscious, with layers of mushroom tomato sauce, pasta, and cream sauce. Greek* kefalotiri *cheese is standard, but I sprinkle the more available Parmesan instead. Either grate the cheese yourself or buy it already grated from the refrigerator case of your market.*

*Makes 4 servings*

Preheat the oven to 350°F. In a large skillet, heat 1 tablespoon of the oil over medium heat. Add the onion and sauté until it begins to turn golden, about 5 minutes. Add the mushrooms and sauté until they begin to brown, about 3 minutes. Add the wine, tomatoes, salt and pepper to taste, oregano, and cinnamon. Bring to a boil over high heat. Reduce the heat to medium and simmer until the sauce is thick, about 10 minutes.

In a large pot of boiling salted water, cook the macaroni until just tender, al dente, about 6 minutes; drain and rinse briefly. Transfer to a bowl and toss with the remaining tablespoon of oil and ¹/₄ cup of the cheese.

To prepare the béchamel sauce, melt the butter in a small saucepan. Add the flour and whisk over low heat 1 minute. Remove from the heat and whisk in the milk. Add salt, pepper, and nutmeg to taste. Simmer over low heat, whisking often, until thick, about 5 minutes. Taste and adjust the seasonings.

Butter a 2-quart casserole and sprinkle with 1 tablespoon of the bread crumbs. Spread half of the macaroni mixture in the casserole. Cover with the mushroom-tomato sauce. Top with the remaining macaroni. Spread the béchamel sauce on top. Sprinkle with the remaining 2 tablespoons bread crumbs and remaining 2 tablespoons cheese. Bake for 30 minutes, or until the casserole begins to bubble and the top is light golden.

# Wild Rice and Shrimp Casserole with Asparagus and Shallots

**One 14¹/₂-ounce can vegetable broth, or 1³/₄ cups vegetable (page 160) or fish stock (page 159)**

**4 cups water**

**1 pound medium or large shrimp in their shells, rinsed**

**1 pound medium or thick asparagus, peeled**

**Salt**

**1 cup wild rice (6 ounces), rinsed and drained**

**2 tablespoons vegetable oil or butter**

**4 large shallots, halved and thinly sliced**

**¹/₂ teaspoon dried thyme**

**Freshly ground black pepper**

**Cayenne pepper**

When you want to put several of your favorite foods in one creation, this is the kind of dish you cook. The shrimp and asparagus look so pretty on the plate with the wild rice. Everyone likes their pure flavors, enhanced by just a nuance of shallots, thyme, and vegetable stock. Best of all, this casserole is easy to prepare. A salad of diced tomatoes, yellow peppers, and cucumbers makes a colorful accompaniment.

*Makes 4 servings*

In a medium saucepan, bring the broth and 2 cups of the water to a simmer. Add the shrimp, cover, and poach over low heat until the shrimp turn pink, 2 to 3 minutes. With a slotted spoon, remove the shrimp, reserving the cooking liquid. Rinse the shrimp with cold water in a strainer, drain, and shell.

Cut off the asparagus tips. Cut each asparagus spear in 1¹/₂-inch pieces, discarding the tough ends (about ¹/₂ inch from end). Bring the shrimp cooking liquid to a boil and add the asparagus. Boil, uncovered, until barely tender, about 2 minutes. With a slotted spoon, remove the asparagus to a strainer, reserving the liquid. Rinse the asparagus with cold water and drain.

To the reserved liquid, add the remaining 2 cups water, bring to boil, and add a pinch of salt. Add the rice, return to a boil, cover, and cook over low heat until the grains begin to swell and are tender, about 50 minutes.

Preheat the oven to 350°F. In a medium sauté pan, heat the oil over medium-low heat. Add the shallots and sauté, stirring, until soft but not brown, about 2 minutes. Remove from the heat. Add the shrimp, asparagus, thyme, and salt, pepper, and cayenne to taste. Mix lightly. With a slotted spoon, transfer the wild rice to the shrimp mixture and toss to combine. Taste and adjust the seasonings.

Transfer the mixture to an oiled 2-quart casserole. Cover and bake 20 minutes to heat through. With each serving, include some broth from the bottom of the casserole.

# Orange Chicken and Pasta Casserole with Soy Sauce and Ginger

**¹/₃ cup strained fresh orange juice**

**3 tablespoons soy sauce**

**2 tablespoons dry white wine**

**2 to 3 tablespoons vegetable oil**

**1 tablespoon honey**

**1 tablespoon finely grated orange zest**

**1 tablespoon grated peeled gingerroot**

**Pinch of cayenne pepper, or to taste**

**1¹/₂ pounds boneless, skinless chicken thighs**

**¹/₂ pound penne or penne rigate**

**1¹/₂ cups frozen peas**

**2 tablespoons chopped fresh Italian parsley**

**Salt and freshly ground black pepper**

To prepare a delicious barbecued chicken casserole, I use grilled marinated chicken as well as its marinade. I bring the marinade to a simmer before mixing it with the other casserole ingredients to be sure it is thoroughly cooked, so there is no worry of salmonella. As the casserole bakes, the marinade has a chance to permeate the pasta and the chicken.

This casserole features my favorite marinade, made of fresh ginger, orange juice, wine, soy sauce, and a touch of honey. I prefer to use boneless, skinless chicken thighs for this casserole because they remain moist and are a snap to prepare. Once the chicken is grilled, all you need to do is cut it into strips. If you like, double the amount of chicken, grill it all, and serve grilled chicken for dinner, using the remaining chicken to make this casserole the next day.

*Makes 4 to 5 servings*

In a shallow dish, mix the orange juice, soy sauce, wine, oil, honey, zest, gingerroot, and cayenne. Add the chicken and turn the pieces to coat. Cover and refrigerate 1 to 2 hours, turning the chicken once or twice while marinating.

Preheat the broiler or grill. Remove the chicken from the marinade, reserving the marinade in a small saucepan. Broil or grill the chicken, brushing twice with the marinade, until the inside is no longer pink, about 4 minutes per side; check by cutting into a thick piece. Transfer to a cutting board.

Preheat the oven to 350°F. In a large pot of boiling salted water, cook the pasta, uncovered, over high heat, stirring occasionally, until tender but firm to the bite, about 8 minutes. Add the peas and heat until separated. Drain well, rinse with cold water, and transfer to a large bowl.

Cut the chicken into strips. Bring the reserved marinade to a simmer, pour over the pasta mixture, and mix well. Add the chicken strips, parsley, and salt and pepper to taste. Transfer the pasta mixture to an oiled 10-cup casserole. Cover and bake 30 minutes, or until heated through. Serve hot.

# Chicken and Shiitake Mushroom Cassoulet

1 **pound dried white beans,** such as great Northern beans (about 2¹⁄₃ cups)

7 cups cold water

1 medium onion, peeled

1 carrot, scraped

One 4¹⁄₂- to 5-pound roasting chicken

2 ounces dried shiitake mushrooms

8 to 10 ounces pearl onions

1 tablespoon olive oil

4 large cloves garlic, chopped

Two 28-ounce cans diced tomatoes, drained

³⁄₄ cup chicken stock (page 157) or broth

1 teaspoon dried thyme

1 bay leaf

1 tablespoon chopped fresh sage (optional)

2 tablespoons chopped fresh basil, or 2 teaspoons dried

Salt and freshly ground black pepper

8 ounces smoked Polish sausage or turkey Polish sausage

¹⁄₄ cup unseasoned bread crumbs

*I*n France cassoulet is one of the best-loved dishes. It is composed of beans layered with meat or poultry, which flavors the beans as the casserole bakes. I like to use roasted chicken rather than the typical duck or goose, which are much fattier. Shiitake mushrooms are a new touch that I add to the standard tomatoes, garlic, and fresh herbs. They contribute fragrance and flavor to the sauce that moistens the casserole.

*Makes 6 to 8 servings*

Sort the beans, discarding any broken ones and any stones. In a large bowl, soak the beans in the cold water overnight. For a quicker method, in a large saucepan, cover the beans with the water, boil 2 minutes, remove from the heat, and let stand for 1 hour.

Rinse and drain the beans and put in a large saucepan. Add enough water to cover by at least 2 inches. Add the onion and carrot, pushing them into the liquid. Cover and bring to a boil over medium heat. Reduce the heat to low and simmer until the beans are just tender, about 1¹⁄₂ hours, adding hot water if needed so that the beans remain covered. Keep the beans in their cooking liquid. (The beans can be cooked 1 day ahead and refrigerated.)

Preheat the oven to 400°F. Place the chicken on a rack in a roasting pan and roast for 1 hour. When cool enough to handle, cut into 8 pieces (drumsticks and thighs separated, each breast cut in half).

In a bowl of hot water to cover, soak the shiitake mushrooms for 20 minutes. Remove and cut into bite-size pieces, discarding the stems.

In a medium saucepan of boiling water, cook the pearl onions 1 minute. Rinse, drain, and peel. In a heavy, large casserole, heat the oil over medium heat. Add the pearl onions and brown lightly, about 3 minutes. Remove with a slotted spoon and set aside. Add the garlic to the casserole and sauté 30 seconds over low heat. Stir in the tomatoes and cook 2 minutes. Add the shiitake mushrooms, stock, thyme, and bay leaf. Cover and simmer 15 minutes. Add the pearl onions and cook until tender, about 15 minutes more. Discard the bay leaf. Add the sage and basil. Taste the sauce and add salt and pepper to taste.

Put the sausage in a medium saucepan, cover with water, and bring to a simmer. Cook over low heat until firm, about 10 minutes. Drain and slice.

Preheat the oven to 375°F. Discard the onion and carrot from the beans. With a slotted spoon, put half of the beans in a 10-cup gratin dish in an even layer. Spoon about half of the mushroom sauce over the beans. Arrange the chicken pieces and sausage slices on the beans. Spoon the remaining beans on top. Reserve the remaining bean liquid. Ladle the remaining mushroom sauce over the beans. Add enough of the reserved bean cooking liquid to come nearly to the top of the beans.

Sprinkle the cassoulet with the bread crumbs and bake about 35 minutes (or 50 minutes if it was made a day ahead and is cold), or until hot and golden brown. Serve from the baking dish.

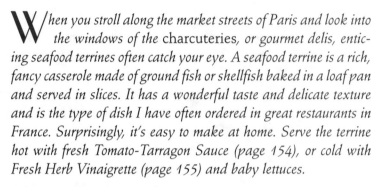

# Terrine with Tomato-Tarragon Sauce

1½ pounds salmon fillets

12 ounces medium shrimp, shelled and deveined

3 large egg whites

1 teaspoon salt

½ teaspoon white pepper

Freshly ground nutmeg

1 cup heavy cream

Tomato-Tarragon Sauce (page 154)

*W*hen you stroll along the market streets of Paris and look into the windows of the charcuteries, or gourmet delis, enticing seafood terrines often catch your eye. A seafood terrine is a rich, fancy casserole made of ground fish or shellfish baked in a loaf pan and served in slices. It has a wonderful taste and delicate texture and is the type of dish I have often ordered in great restaurants in France. Surprisingly, it's easy to make at home. Serve the terrine hot with fresh Tomato-Tarragon Sauce (page 154), or cold with Fresh Herb Vinaigrette (page 155) and baby lettuces.

*Makes 5 to 6 servings*

Remove any skin and bones from the salmon. Cut the fish into 1-inch pieces. Cut two-thirds of the shrimp into thick slices and refrigerate. Reserve the remaining whole shrimp for grinding with the salmon.

In a food processor, grind half the salmon with the reserved whole shrimp until very finely ground. Add 1 egg white and process until blended. Transfer to a bowl. In the food processor, grind the remaining salmon and a second egg white. Leave the mixture in the processor. Return the first mixture to the processor. Add the third egg white, salt, pepper, and nutmeg to taste. Process until thoroughly blended and very smooth. Transfer to a bowl, cover, and refrigerate 30 minutes. Refrigerate the work bowl of the processor also.

Preheat the oven to 350°F. Butter a 6-cup terrine mold or loaf pan. Line the base of the pan with waxed paper or parchment paper and butter the paper.

Return the cold fish mixture to the food processor. With the machine running, gradually pour in the cream in a slow, steady stream. Taste and adjust the seasonings; if adding more seasoning, process until mixed. Transfer the mixture to a bowl. Thoroughly mix in the shrimp slices.

Spoon the mixture into the mold. Pack the mixture in the mold well, pushing it into the corners. Smooth the top. Tap the mold on a table to be sure the mixture is packed down. Cover the mixture with buttered paper and top with a lid, or cover with 2 layers of foil, sealing the top around the edge of the pan. (The unbaked terrine can be kept, covered, up to 4 hours in the refrigerator.)

Set the mold in a larger pan and fill the pan with very hot water about halfway up the sides of the mold. Bake about 35 minutes, or until set; a skewer inserted into the mixture and left in for 10 to 15 seconds should come out hot to the touch. Remove the mold from the pan of water and let sit about 10 minutes before unmolding, or refrigerate if serving cold.

To serve, unmold the terrine onto a platter or board; drain off any liquid. With a sharp knife, cut carefully into ¹/₂-inch slices. Serve with sauce or vinaigrette.

# Zucchini Gratin with Potatoes, Tomatoes, and Parmesan

**12 ounces boiling potatoes, unpeeled (about 3 potatoes)**

**Salt**

**12 ounces zucchini (about 2 zucchini)**

**5¹/₂ ounces ripe plum tomatoes (about 6 large plum tomatoes)**

**Freshly ground black pepper**

**3 tablespoons olive oil**

**2 large cloves garlic, minced**

**2 teaspoons fresh thyme, or ³/₄ teaspoon dried**

**2 tablespoons chopped fresh oregano, or 1¹/₂ teaspoons dried**

**2 tablespoons freshly grated Parmesan cheese**

*A*lternating slices of vegetables make a green, white, and red pattern for this picture-perfect vegetable casserole. A sprinkling of fresh herbs, garlic, and Parmesan ensures that everyone will love the flavor, too. Use a large gratin dish or arrange the vegetables in individual gratin dishes. For a most attractive presentation, choose small potatoes, medium zucchini, and large Roma tomatoes so that the vegetable slices will be similar in diameter. This casserole is inspired by the tians of Provence, a type of vegetable gratin seasoned with olive oil, garlic, Parmesan cheese, and often eggs.

*Makes 4 servings*

In a medium saucepan, cover the potatoes with water and add a pinch of salt. Bring to a boil, cover, and cook over low heat until nearly tender, about 20 minutes. With a slotted spoon, remove the potatoes to a bowl, reserving the cooking water in the pan. Add the whole zucchini to the cooking water and return to a boil. Cook, uncovered, over medium heat until nearly tender, about 5 minutes. Drain, discarding the cooking water, and rinse with cold water. Cut the potatoes and zucchini into slices about ¹/₂ inch thick, keeping each vegetable separate.

Preheat the oven to 400°F. Cut the tomatoes into rounds about ¹/₄ inch thick, discarding the ends. Remove the seeds from the slices.

Oil a 14 × 8-inch oval gratin dish or other large, shallow baking dish. Arrange rows of overlapping potato, zucchini, and tomato slices in a single layer in the pan, making every other slice a tomato slice. Fill any spaces remaining in the dish with smaller slices or half slices of the vegetables. Sprinkle the vegetables with salt and pepper.

In the pan used to cook the vegetables, heat the oil. Add the garlic and cook 30 seconds over low heat. Remove from the heat and stir in the thyme and oregano. Pour the herb oil into a ramekin. Using a teaspoon, spoon it evenly over the vegetables. Sprinkle with the Parmesan cheese. Bake about 15 minutes, or until the vegetables are very tender and the cheese melts. Serve hot or warm from the baking dish.

*Note: This recipe calls for a generous amount of each vegetable so that you'll have enough to alternate them, since everyone overlaps them in a slightly different manner. If you have extra slices, you can arrange them in a separate small gratin dish, sprinkle with a little oil and cheese, and bake them.*

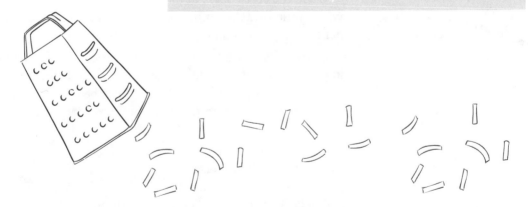

# Salmon and Rice Baked with Garlic and Saffron

**¹/₈ teaspoon saffron threads**

**¹/₃ cup boiling water**

**3 tablespoons olive oil**

**2 medium onions, chopped**

**4 large cloves garlic, minced**

**5 cups cooked rice**

**¹/₂ teaspoon dried thyme**

**Salt and freshly ground black pepper**

**1 pound skinless salmon fillet**

*This has been a big hit. Also works well with smoked salmon.*

This entrée demonstrates what a scrumptious casserole you can make with a small number of ingredients. It's composed of a lightly sautéed salmon fillet layered with saffron rice and then baked. I find that jasmine rice gives the casserole a superior flavor, but any type of cooked rice will be fine. Cook the rice according to the package directions.

Serve this casserole with a simply cooked green vegetable. My favorite choices are asparagus, green beans, or sugar snap peas.

*Makes 4 servings*

Preheat the oven to 350°F. Put the saffron in a measuring cup, add the boiling water, and let stand for 15 minutes.

In a nonstick skillet, heat 2 tablespoons of the oil over medium heat. Add the onions and sauté until they just begin to turn golden, about 7 minutes. Add the garlic and sauté 30 seconds. Transfer to a large bowl, reserving the skillet.

Add the cooked rice to the bowl of onions and mix gently with a fork. Add the saffron mixture, thyme, and salt and pepper to taste; mix gently.

In the skillet used for cooking the onions, heat the remaining tablespoon of oil. Add the salmon and sauté over medium heat 2 minutes per side; the fish will not be cooked through. Remove the salmon from the pan and flake into large pieces, removing any bones.

Transfer half of the rice mixture to an oiled 2-quart casserole. Set the salmon pieces on top and sprinkle with salt and pepper to taste. Top with the remaining rice mixture. Cover and bake 40 minutes, or until heated through.

# Casseroles from the Pantry

*Salmon, Noodle, and Broccoli Casserole with Salsa*

*Rice with Lima Beans and Dill*

*Double Tomato Macaroni Casserole with Peppers*

*My Mother's Tuna and Potato Casserole*

*Pinto Bean and Corn Casserole in a Flash*

*Easy Tortilla Casserole with Vegetables and Cheese*

*Spinach and Sausage Casserole with Brown Rice*

Even when you don't have time to shop for fresh ingredients, you can easily make a casserole from foods you have on hand, whether in your cupboard or your freezer. Grains and pasta are the best example of items in everyone's pantry and are an easy foundation for a nutritious meal. If you keep plenty of healthful, fine-quality pantry foods on hand, the casseroles you prepare from the staples you have can be varied and interesting. Naturally, the items you stock will depend on your taste and your space.

Many traditional casserole ingredients are pantry items. After all, refrigerators didn't always exist, and people developed methods such as drying and canning to preserve foods for those times when there was no fresh harvest. Throughout history people used these ingredients to prepare casseroles. Some casseroles that depend mainly on pantry items, like American baked beans and French cassoulet, have been made for hundreds of years.

Today there are many delicious seasonings and pantry foods available from around the world to use in casseroles. There's no reason for casseroles from the cupboard to be monotonous. For a list of foods I find useful to have on hand for quick casseroles, see page xv.

Here is an example of how to easily turn pantry items into a casserole: Cook pasta and frozen vegetables together, then drain and mix with canned diced tomatoes, a little oil, and dried thyme and oregano for a quick entrée. You can add bottled roasted peppers, oil-packed sun-dried tomatoes, or cayenne pepper for a touch of heat. Either warm the dish in a sauté pan as a stovetop casserole, or top it with Parmesan cheese and bake it briefly until the cheese melts.

If you're in the mood for a grain dish, bake rice with a frozen vegetable and a dried herb, as in Rice with Lima Beans and Dill. This casserole is flavored with sautéed onion and canned vegetable broth and is delicious as a main course or side dish. You can even use stale bread or tortillas to prepare casseroles by moistening them with broth, tomato sauce, or sautéed vegetables, then baking the mixture as you would for bread stuffing, as in recipes like Zucchini-Mushroom Casserole with Pecans (page 56) and Easy Tortilla Casserole with Vegetables and Cheese.

Canned fish make tasty casseroles too, especially when combined with mashed potatoes or noodles. For a simple-to-make fish casserole that I learned from my mother, I mix mashed potatoes with canned tuna or salmon, eggs, and a little sour cream, and then I bake the mixture (page 98). This tasty casserole is a favorite with children.

If you have a chance to prepare your own pantry items, such as roasted peppers, chicken stock, and oil-packed sun-dried tomatoes, your casseroles will be even better.

# Salmon, Noodle, and Broccoli Casserole with Salsa

3 tablespoons olive oil

2 large onions, halved and sliced

2 large cloves garlic, chopped

One 10-ounce package frozen broccoli

Salt and freshly ground black pepper

8 ounces medium noodles

3 tablespoons bottled mild green salsa, or to taste

One 6-ounce can red salmon, drained and flaked

Chopped green onions for garnish

Keep green salsa, made of tomatillos, or red tomato salsa in your pantry to flavor casseroles, not just to accompany them. Instead of using white sauce or canned condensed soup, use salsa along with sautéed onions and garlic to flavor this lighter version of the traditional noodle and canned salmon casserole. Adding frozen broccoli is an easy way to slip in some valuable nutrients and good taste too. Red salmon gives the finest flavor, but the casserole also is good when made with less expensive pink salmon.

*Makes 4 servings*

In a large skillet, heat 2 tablespoons of the oil over medium heat. Add the onions and sauté 3 minutes. Cover and cook, stirring often, until golden, about 10 minutes. Add the garlic and sauté 1 minute. Remove from heat.

Preheat the oven to 350°F. In a medium saucepan with enough boiling water to cover, cook the broccoli, uncovered, until just tender, about 3 minutes. Drain, rinse with cold water, and drain well. Chop the broccoli. Add to the pan of onions and sprinkle with salt and pepper to taste.

In a large pot of boiling salted water, cook the noodles, uncovered, over high heat until just tender, al dente, about 5 minutes. Drain, rinse with cold water, and drain well.

In a large bowl, combine the noodles and broccoli mixture. Add the salsa to taste. Oil a 2-quart casserole and spoon in half the noodle mixture. Top with the salmon, then the remaining noodle mixture. Sprinkle with the remaining oil. Bake 30 minutes. Serve hot, sprinkled with the green onions.

# Rice with Lima Beans and Dill

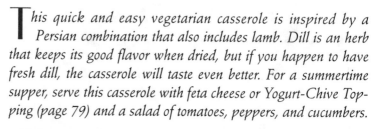

2 to 3 tablespoons
vegetable oil

1 medium onion,
finely chopped

1½ cups long-grain rice

One 14-ounce can
vegetable or chicken
broth (1¾ cups)

1½ cups water

One 10-ounce package
frozen lima beans

Salt and freshly ground
black pepper

2 tablespoons snipped fresh
dill, or 2 teaspoons
dried

This quick and easy vegetarian casserole is inspired by a Persian combination that also includes lamb. Dill is an herb that keeps its good flavor when dried, but if you happen to have fresh dill, the casserole will taste even better. For a summertime supper, serve this casserole with feta cheese or Yogurt-Chive Topping (page 79) and a salad of tomatoes, peppers, and cucumbers.

*Makes 4 to 6 servings*

Preheat the oven to 350°F. In a sauté pan or large skillet, heat the oil over medium-low heat. Add the onion and cook, stirring often, until soft but not brown, about 7 minutes. Add the rice and sauté, stirring, 2 minutes. Transfer the mixture to an oiled 2-quart casserole.

In a medium saucepan, bring the broth and water to a boil and add the lima beans. Return to a boil and cook until the beans are separated, about 2 minutes. Spoon the lima beans with their liquid over the rice mixture. Add a pinch of salt and pepper. Cover tightly and bake for 30 minutes, or until the rice is just tender.

Using a fork, fluff the rice and gently stir in the dill. Taste and adjust the seasonings. Serve hot.

# Double Tomato Macaroni Casserole with Peppers

8 ounces large elbow
macaroni

3 tablespoons olive oil

2 teaspoons dried oregano

2 large cloves garlic,
minced

Pinch of cayenne pepper

1/4 cup dry-packed sun-
dried tomatoes

1/4 cup plus 2 tablespoons
grated Parmesan cheese

Salt and freshly ground
black pepper

1 pound fresh tomatoes,
diced, or one
14 1/2-ounce can diced
tomatoes, drained

3/4 cup roasted red bell
pepper strips
(homemade, see page
xvii, or from a jar)

Everyone loves to make this kind of casserole because it's practically effortless. The directions are essentially to take a few
ingredients from your pantry, mix them, and bake the mixture in
the oven. The only food that needs precooking is the pasta. With
sun-dried tomatoes, roasted peppers from a jar, olive oil, and a
sprinkling of Parmesan, you will see that a pasta casserole does
not need a sauce to be flavorful.

*Makes 4 to 5 main-course servings;*
*6 side-dish servings*

Preheat the oven to 350°F. In a large pot of boiling salted water,
cook the pasta 7 minutes. Meanwhile, in a large bowl, mix
2 tablespoons of the oil with the oregano, garlic, and cayenne;
let stand.

After the pasta has cooked 7 minutes, add the dried tomatoes and cook until the pasta is just tender, al dente, about
2 minutes. Drain and rinse well with cold water. Remove the
dried tomatoes from the pasta and finely dice.

Add the pasta to the bowl of garlic mixture and toss. Add
1/4 cup of the cheese and salt and pepper to taste. Add the fresh
or canned tomatoes, sun-dried tomatoes, and roasted peppers
and mix lightly. Taste and adjust the seasonings.

Transfer the pasta mixture to an oiled 2-quart casserole.
Top with the remaining tablespoon of oil and 2 tablespoons of
cheese. Bake, uncovered, 30 minutes, or until the top is lightly
browned.

# My Mother's Tuna and Potato Casserole

3 tablespoons vegetable oil

1 large onion, chopped

1 pound boiling potatoes, unpeeled

Salt

1/4 cup warm nonfat, low-fat, or whole milk

1/4 cup plain whole, low-fat, or nonfat yogurt

One 6-ounce can tuna in water, drained

2 large eggs

1/2 teaspoon dried thyme

Freshly ground black pepper

Cayenne pepper

About 1/2 cup unseasoned bread crumbs

This is an updated version of an old-fashioned casserole. My mother used to mash the potatoes with butter and enrich the casserole with sour cream, but since then she has lightened it, and so have I. It's still a family favorite and is also good when made with canned salmon instead of tuna. Serve it with sliced tomatoes and cucumbers.

*Makes 4 servings*

Preheat the oven to 350°F. In a large skillet, heat 2 tablespoons of the oil over medium heat. Add the onion and sauté, stirring often, until golden, about 7 minutes.

In a large saucepan, cover the potatoes with water, add a pinch of salt, and bring to a boil. Cover and simmer over low heat until very tender, about 35 minutes. Drain and let sit until cool enough to handle but not cold.

Peel the potatoes. Cut each into a few pieces, put in a large bowl, and mash. Beat in the warm milk. Stir in the yogurt, tuna, eggs, thyme, sautéed onion, and salt, pepper, and cayenne to taste. Mix well.

Grease an 8-inch casserole and sprinkle the bottom and sides with bread crumbs. Add the tuna mixture. Top with more bread crumbs and drizzle with the remaining tablespoon of oil. Bake for 45 minutes, or until firm. Serve hot.

# Pinto Bean and Corn Casserole in a Flash

**One 15-ounce can pinto beans, drained**

**One 10-ounce package frozen corn, cooked and drained**

**One 14½-ounce can diced tomatoes, drained**

**½ teaspoon dried oregano**

**¼ teaspoon dried hot red pepper flakes, or to taste**

**½ cup diced roasted red peppers (homemade, see page xvii, or from a jar)**

**Salt and freshly ground black pepper to taste**

This is the right choice as a last-minute casserole when everyone is hungry and you need to have a hearty main course ready in a jiffy. Heat the beans, corn, tomatoes, and seasonings on top of the stove or, if you prefer, put them in a covered casserole and heat the casserole in the microwave.

As a hearty variation, you can add a 1-pound can of meaty chili and serve the casserole with rice. For an even faster casserole, use a 15-ounce can of corn kernels instead of frozen corn.

*Makes 4 servings*

In a medium saucepan combine all the ingredients. Cover and cook over medium heat, stirring occasionally, until heated through, about 5 minutes. Taste and adjust the seasonings.

# Easy Tortilla Casserole with Vegetables and Cheese

2 tablespoons vegetable oil

1 onion, halved and thinly sliced

2 cloves garlic, chopped

One 28-ounce can diced tomatoes, drained

1 teaspoon dried oregano

One 1-pound package frozen mixed vegetables containing lima beans and corn, cooked and drained

Salt and freshly ground black pepper

Hot sauce to taste

5 corn tortillas (6-inch diameter), halved and cut into strips ¼ inch wide

½ cup shredded Monterey Jack cheese

¼ cup freshly grated Parmesan cheese

Mexican cooks use up stale tortillas in casseroles, just as Americans use up old bread in stuffings. Traditionally these casseroles, called chilaquiles, require frying the tortillas. This step is not needed for this lighter version, which is kept moist by tomato sauce. The tortillas are cut into strips like noodles, and the casserole is assembled in layers, like a very quick lasagna. You can use stale or fresh tortillas, depending on what you have on hand. If you like, make the casserole with fat-free tortillas, a recent arrival in our markets.

*Makes 4 to 6 servings*

Preheat the oven to 350°F. In a large skillet, heat the oil over medium heat. Add the onion and sauté until lightly browned, about 7 minutes. Stir in the garlic, then the tomatoes and oregano. Cook, uncovered, until the sauce is thick, about 10 minutes. Stir in the cooked mixed vegetables. Season to taste with salt, pepper, and hot sauce.

Lightly oil an 8-inch square baking dish and a piece of foil fit to cover. Spread half the vegetable mixture in the dish. Top with half the tortilla strips. Sprinkle with half the Monterey Jack cheese. Repeat the layers. Cover and bake for 30 minutes. Sprinkle with the Parmesan cheese. Bake, uncovered, 5 to 10 minutes, or until the top begins to brown. Let stand 10 minutes before serving.

# Spinach and Sausage Casserole with Brown Rice

**1 tablespoon vegetable oil**

**3 cloves garlic, minced**

**6 ounces cooked smoked sausage, sliced**

**One 14¹/₂-ounce can vegetable or chicken broth (1³/₄ cups)**

**2 cups quick-cooking brown rice**

**One 10-ounce package frozen leaf spinach**

**Salt and freshly ground black pepper**

**3 tablespoons freshly grated Parmesan cheese**

I f you keep sausage and frozen spinach in your kitchen, this casserole is a snap to make. Use your family's favorite sausage—meat, turkey, or chicken. Substitute diced peppers, onions, and celery for the spinach to make a speedy version of jambalaya. If you prefer a vegetarian rice and spinach casserole, omit the sausages or use the vegetarian sausages now available at some markets. If you don't have brown rice, you can use quick-cooking white rice. Serve this casserole with a salad of grated carrots and dried cranberries dressed lightly with oil and vinegar.

*Makes 4 servings*

Preheat the oven to 375°F. In a large sauté pan, heat the oil over medium heat. Add the garlic and sauté 30 seconds. Add the sausage and sauté, stirring, 30 seconds.

Add the broth and rice and stir once. Add the spinach. Cover and bring to a boil over medium-high heat, breaking up the spinach from time to time. Reduce the heat to low, cover tightly, and simmer, without stirring, until the rice is tender, about 10 minutes. Fluff the rice gently with a fork. Season to taste with salt and pepper.

Transfer the rice mixture to a lightly oiled 2-quart casserole. Sprinkle with the Parmesan cheese. Bake, uncovered, for 20 minutes, or until the cheese melts and browns lightly.

# Casseroles in Minutes

*Spicy Spirals with Turkey and Mushrooms*

*Chicken Casserole with Potatoes, Mushrooms, and Onions*

*Lima Beans with Sausage, Tomatoes, and Raisins*

*Ten-Minute Beef and Bulgur Wheat Casserole with Chickpeas and Red Peppers*

*Black Bean and Rice Casserole with Hot Caribbean Pesto*

*Speedy Corn and Pepper Casserole*

*Easy Leek Gratin*

*Carrot and Pineapple Tsimmes with Ginger*

Casseroles can be quick and easy to prepare if you choose the right ingredients and cooking techniques. To prepare main-course casseroles in a short time, select meats that naturally cook quickly, such as ground beef, chicken, or turkey; boneless, skinless chicken thighs or breasts; turkey breast slices; or thin steaks. Most types of fish cook in just a few minutes; fastest of all are thin fillets, scallops, and shrimp. Once cooked, seafood needs only to be briefly heated in a casserole. Even frozen shrimp and scallops can be made into casseroles in short order, because they thaw rapidly.

Consider not only the cooking time but also the preparation time before the food goes into the pot. Buy ingredients that have been "cleaned," such as shelled shrimp, skinless fish fillets, well-trimmed steaks, and other boneless cuts of meat. Or make use of convenience foods—buy roasted chicken, turkey, or beef at the deli or the market and turn it into tasty entrées like Ten-Minute Beef and Bulgur Wheat Casserole with Chickpeas and Red Peppers. Many of the foods suggested in "Casseroles from the Pantry" (page 93) also help save time.

Take advantage of the prepared fresh vegetables offered at the market. Instead of chopping onions, buy ready-diced onions, which are available fresh or frozen. You can also purchase sliced mushrooms, shredded carrots, peeled baby carrots, shredded cabbage, cleaned spinach, squash cut into sticks, ready-to-cook asparagus spears, and chopped garlic. Make liberal use of frozen vegetables and canned beans for quick, satisfying, nutritious casseroles, such as Speedy Corn and Pepper Casserole. If you must chop or shred vegetables, consider using a food processor.

When shopping for pasta, note that the cooking times of pastas vary enormously. They can range from 1 minute for some kinds of angel-hair pasta to 12 minutes for some thick shapes; even spaghetti's cooking time differs from one brand to another. Flavored pasta helps save time too; your casserole will already be seasoned, and you don't need to add many spices. Grains have great variation in cooking times as well. White rice cooks in 14 to 20 minutes, and brown rice in about 40 minutes. Fortunately, both white and brown rice come in quick-cooking versions that are ready in 10 minutes.

When you are racing the clock, don't spend time making sauces. Use canned diced tomatoes, prepared tomato sauce, roasted peppers in a jar, or a small amount of flavored oil such as garlic or basil oil to moisten your casseroles. Choose fast cooking techniques. When a recipe calls for cooked vegetables, for example, remember that boiling vegetables takes less time than steaming.

Whenever possible, combine ingredients in the pot if you need to precook them. Cook pasta or rice together with vegetables. Simply add frozen vegetables or diced fresh ones to pasta or rice as it cooks, adding them according to their cooking times.

Some casseroles, such as Chicken Casserole with Potatoes, Mushrooms, and Onions, save on effort, requiring little precooking or other preparation. Most of the time needed to make these types of casseroles is almost-unattended baking time.

# Spicy Spirals with Turkey and Mushrooms

2 to 3 tablespoons olive oil

1 large onion, minced

3 large cloves garlic, minced

8 ounces ground turkey

One 14½-ounce can diced tomatoes, drained

2 tablespoons tomato paste

½ cup canned chicken broth

1 teaspoon dried oregano

½ teaspoon hot red pepper flakes

Salt and freshly ground black pepper

One 6-ounce package sliced fresh mushrooms (about 3 cups)

1 pound pasta spirals or fusilli

8 ounces green or yellow zucchini (2 small zucchini), diced

*A*ttractive spiral-shaped pasta, often called fusilli, catches every morsel of the peppery turkey-mushroom-tomato sauce. Zucchini cooks in the pot with the pasta, so you have less to clean. The brief baking helps the taste of the sauce permeate the pasta.

*If you have roasted turkey or chicken on hand, omit the ground turkey from the sauce and stir 1 to 2 cups diced cooked turkey or chicken into the finished sauce.*

*Makes 4 to 6 servings*

Preheat the oven to 350°F. In a heavy, medium sauté pan, heat 2 tablespoons of the oil over medium-high heat. Add the onion and sauté, stirring often, until softened slightly, about 2 minutes. Add the garlic and turkey and sauté, breaking up the meat with a fork, until it changes color, about 3 minutes. Add the tomatoes, tomato paste, broth, oregano, red pepper flakes, and salt and pepper to taste and bring to a boil, stirring. Add the mushrooms. Cover and cook over medium-low heat, stirring occasionally, 8 to 10 minutes.

Meanwhile, in a large pot of boiling salted water, cook the pasta, uncovered, 5 minutes. Add the zucchini and boil until the pasta is tender but firm to the bite, about 2 minutes. Drain the pasta and zucchini and transfer to a 3-quart casserole. Add the sauce and toss. Taste and adjust the seasonings; add the remaining tablespoon of oil if desired. Cover and bake 15 minutes, or until hot.

# Chicken Casserole with Potatoes, Mushrooms, and Onions

**1 tablespoon ground cumin**

**¾ teaspoon ground turmeric**

**Freshly ground black pepper**

**3 pounds boiling potatoes, peeled and sliced ⅜ inch thick**

**Salt**

**3 pounds chicken pieces**

**8 ounces mushrooms, quartered**

**1 pound onions, halved and sliced**

*This delicious entrée is ideal for entertaining as well as for family dinners. And it's easy to prepare; you just assemble the ingredients in one roasting pan. Although it bakes for an hour and a half, the baking time is unattended and none of the ingredients need precooking. The Yemenite mixture of cumin and turmeric gives the dish its wonderful flavor and aroma and its warm, golden color. Serve this with a Mediterranean appetizer salad of diced tomatoes, cucumbers, and parsley with olive oil and fresh lemon juice.*

*Makes 6 servings*

Preheat the oven to 375°F. In a small bowl, mix the cumin, turmeric, and ½ teaspoon of the pepper. Lightly oil a medium roasting pan. Spread the potatoes in it, sprinkle with salt and pepper to taste, and toss to coat. Top with the chicken pieces, season both sides with salt, and rub the spice mixture into the chicken. Top with the mushrooms, then the onions. Cover with foil and bake 1 hour 25 minutes. Uncover and bake for 15 minutes, or until the chicken is tender. Juices should no longer be pink when the thickest part of the thigh is pierced; the potatoes should be tender as well.

Just before serving, uncover and broil 4 inches from the heat until browned on top, 3 to 4 minutes.

# Lima Beans with Sausage, Tomatoes, and Raisins

**One 1-pound package frozen lima beans**

**1 tablespoon olive oil**

**4 green onions, white and green parts, chopped**

**2 large cloves garlic, chopped**

**One 14½-ounce can diced tomatoes, drained**

**2 teaspoons sweet paprika**

**½ teaspoon ground cumin**

**⅛ teaspoon ground cinnamon**

**½ cup water**

**½ pound smoked sausage or beef frankfurters, cut into 1-inch pieces**

**¼ cup dark raisins**

**Salt and freshly ground black pepper**

The idea for this easy, savory entrée came from a Spanish dish made with fava beans and sausages spiced with cumin and cinnamon. For an impromptu supper, I substitute common items likely to be in the kitchen—beef frankfurters and frozen lima beans. You can use any sausage you like. To give this dish a Spanish character, I put a little cumin and cinnamon in the sauce. Serve this casserole with rice or crusty bread.

*Makes 4 servings*

In a wide casserole or sauté pan containing enough boiling water to cover, cook the lima beans until just tender, about 5 minutes. Drain and set aside.

In the casserole, heat the oil over medium-low heat. Add the chopped green onions and garlic and sauté 1 minute, stirring. Add the tomatoes, raise the heat to medium, and cook 3 minutes. Stir in the paprika, cumin, and cinnamon, add the water, and bring to a boil. Add the sausage and raisins, cover, and simmer over low heat for 5 minutes. Add the lima beans, cover, and heat through, 3 to 5 minutes. Season to taste with salt and pepper.

# Ten-Minute Beef and Bulgur Wheat Casserole with Chickpeas and Red Peppers

**1 tablespoon olive oil**

**1 large red bell pepper, cut into 1-inch squares**

**1¹/₃ cups bulgur wheat**

**2²/₃ cups hot water**

**One 15¹/₂-ounce can chickpeas, drained**

**1 to 2 cups finely diced grilled steak**

**Salt and freshly ground black pepper**

**2 tablespoons shredded fresh basil, or 2 teaspoons dried**

*C*asseroles like this one present a healthful and economical way to use meat. When you have a small amount of leftover roast beef or grilled steak, use it here. In this casserole the meat flavors the grain and beans. With the sweet red bell pepper, chickpeas, and fresh basil, this entrée is colorful, tasty, and very easy to prepare. If you have grilled or roasted chicken or turkey in your refrigerator, you can substitute them for the beef.

*Makes 4 servings*

In a large sauté pan, heat the oil over high heat. Add the bell pepper and sauté until it begins to soften, about 2 minutes. Add the bulgur wheat, reduce the heat to low, and stir briefly. Add the hot water and bring to a boil. Cover and cook over low heat 8 minutes. Add the chickpeas, steak, salt and pepper to taste, and the dried basil if using. Cover and cook over low heat until the steak and chickpeas are heated through, about 2 minutes. Add the fresh basil if using. Taste and adjust the seasonings. Serve hot.

# Black Bean and Rice Casserole with Hot Caribbean Pesto

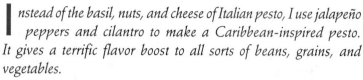

1/4 cup plus 1 tablespoon olive oil

1 medium onion, sliced

2 red, yellow, or green bell peppers, cut into strips

1 teaspoon ground cumin

One 15-ounce can black beans, drained

1/4 cup water

Salt and freshly ground black pepper

2 jalapeño peppers

2 large cloves garlic, peeled

1 cup cilantro

3 cups cooked white rice

Hot sauce (optional)

2 tablespoons chopped green onion (optional)

*Instead of the basil, nuts, and cheese of Italian pesto, I use jalapeño peppers and cilantro to make a Caribbean-inspired pesto. It gives a terrific flavor boost to all sorts of beans, grains, and vegetables.*

*This casserole makes a wonderful vegetarian entrée, but if you wish, you can add 2 cups of diced cooked chicken or turkey to the casserole mixture before baking it. If you don't have cooked rice on hand, use quick-cooking white or brown rice.*

*Makes 4 servings*

Preheat the oven to 350°F. In a large sauté pan, heat 2 table-spoons of the oil over medium heat. Add the onion and bell peppers and sauté until the onion begins to turn golden, about 7 minutes. Add the cumin, reduce the heat to low, and stir 1 minute. Add the beans, water, and salt and pepper to taste. Stir and bring to a boil. Cover and simmer until the peppers are tender, about 5 minutes.

Meanwhile, make the pesto. (Wear gloves when handling hot peppers.) Remove the seeds and ribs from the jalapeño peppers if desired. In a food processor, mince the peppers and garlic until fine. Add the cilantro, remaining 3 tablespoons of oil, and a pinch of salt and process until blended.

In a large bowl, gently toss the bean mixture with the cooked rice. Add the pesto and mix gently with a fork. Taste and adjust the seasonings, adding hot sauce to taste if desired. Transfer the mixture to a lightly oiled 2-quart casserole. Cover and bake 15 minutes, or until the casserole is hot. Serve sprinkled with green onion if desired.

# Speedy Corn and Pepper Casserole

2 tablespoons vegetable oil

2 medium onions, chopped

2 large red or green bell
peppers, diced

1 pound frozen corn
kernels (3¹⁄₃ cups)

One 14¹⁄₂-ounce can diced
tomatoes, drained well

1 teaspoon sugar

Salt and freshly ground
black pepper

¹⁄₄ teaspoon cayenne
pepper, or to taste

This easy casserole is based on the Louisiana specialty corn maquechou, *in which corn kernels are cut from the cob and simmered with onions, green peppers, tomatoes, and butter. For this lighter rendition, I use a touch of oil instead of butter and a higher proportion of the aromatic vegetables, onions and peppers. Using frozen corn is much quicker than cutting it off the cob; choose white or yellow corn according to your preference. You can prepare this convenient casserole two days ahead and keep it in the refrigerator.*

*Makes 4 servings*

Preheat the oven to 350°F. In a large skillet, heat the oil over medium-high heat and stir in the onions and bell peppers. Cover and cook, stirring occasionally, until softened, about 5 minutes.

In a 2-quart casserole, combine the onion-pepper mixture with the corn, tomatoes, sugar, salt and black pepper to taste, and the cayenne. Mix well. Cover and bake 30 minutes, or until the corn is tender. Taste and adjust the seasonings. Serve hot.

# Easy Leek Gratin

**1¹/₂ pounds medium-sized leeks**

**2 tablespoons butter, melted**

**Salt and freshly ground black pepper**

**¹/₂ cup coarsely grated Gruyère cheese**

**¹/₄ cup coarsely chopped walnuts or pecans**

**2 tablespoons unseasoned bread crumbs**

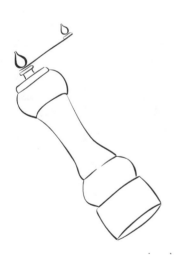

No sauce is needed for this quick side-dish casserole. A simple topping of walnuts, bread crumbs, and cheese makes this gratin delicious. Serve it with roast chicken or sautéed turkey cutlets and, to complete the menu, a salad of diced tomatoes and cucumbers.

*Makes 4 servings*

Starting about 1 inch from the root end of the leeks, split them in four lengthwise, leaving them joined at the root end, and cutting toward the top. Soak the leeks in cold water to cover for 5 minutes. Rinse well to remove any remaining sand. Use the white and light green parts only; save the dark parts for making vegetable broth.

Preheat the oven to 425°F. Butter a shallow 5-cup gratin dish or other heavy baking dish.

In a large saucepan of boiling salted water, cook the leeks, uncovered, until they are just tender when pierced with a small, sharp knife, 7 to 10 minutes. Drain the leeks gently, rinse with cold water, and drain well.

Finish splitting the leeks toward the root end. Cut each leek into 3-inch lengths, pat dry, and arrange in the baking dish in a single layer. Drizzle with 1 tablespoon of the melted butter and sprinkle with a pinch of salt and pepper. Mix the cheese, nuts, and bread crumbs and sprinkle evenly on top. Drizzle with the remaining tablespoon of melted butter.

Bake about 8 minutes, or until the cheese melts. If the topping is not brown, broil just until lightly browned, about 1 minute, checking often. Serve hot from the baking dish.

# Carrot and Pineapple Tsimmes with Ginger

**One 12-ounce package fresh pineapple, or one 16-ounce can pineapple chunks in juice**

**1 tablespoon cornstarch**

**1 pound carrots, scraped and sliced ½ inch thick**

**1 cup water**

**Pinch of salt**

**2 tablespoons honey**

**1 tablespoon chopped peeled gingerroot**

**One 8-ounce can sliced water chestnuts, rinsed and drained**

A specialty of eastern European Jewish cooking, tsimmes *is a casserole of carrots, sweet potatoes, or other sweet vegetables, often combined with dried fruit. It can be a side vegetable dish, or it can contain meat for serving as a main course. Many families enjoy* tsimmes *as a traditional dish for the Jewish New Year because it symbolizes sweetness for the coming year. In this zesty twist on an old favorite, I like to pair the carrots with fresh pineapple and accent the dish with gingerroot and water chestnuts. The savory-sweet casserole makes a marvelous companion for roasted chicken or turkey.*

*Makes 4 servings*

Preheat the oven to 350°F. Drain the pineapple, reserving 2 tablespoons of the juice, and mix the juice with the cornstarch in a cup to blend.

In a medium saucepan, combine the carrots with the water and salt. Bring to a boil, cover, and cook over low heat until just tender, 10 to 12 minutes. Remove the carrots with a slotted spoon. Add the honey and gingerroot to the carrot cooking water and bring to a simmer, stirring. Add the cornstarch mixture to the simmering liquid, stirring. Cook over medium-low heat, stirring, until the sauce comes to a simmer and thickens. Remove from the heat and stir in the carrots, water chestnuts, and pineapple.

Transfer the mixture to a lightly oiled 2-quart casserole. Bake 20 minutes, or until bubbling.

# Stovetop Casseroles

*Moroccan-Style Ratatouille*

*Hot Orzo with Onions*

*Black-eyed Peas with Rice and Peppers*

*Three-Bean Casserole with Tomatoes and Garlic*

*Skillet Steak with Baby Corn, Mint, and Chiles*

*Fideos with Turkey, Summer Squash, and Cumin-Tomato Sauce*

*Sweet-and-Sour Apricot Chicken*

We tend to think of casseroles as oven-baked dishes. The truth is that wonderful casseroles can be cooked in a Dutch oven, skillet, or sauté pan set on a burner. That's how casseroles were cooked before ovens were common. Indeed, that's how casseroles are still made in countries where many homes lack an oven. Certain foods fare better in stovetop casseroles than in oven-baked ones. Stovetop casseroles are particularly suited to tender, quick-cooking cuts of meat, such as strips of turkey breast or steak, as in Skillet Steak with Baby Corn, Mint, and Chiles. By sautéeing these meats in a frying pan, then creating a casserole by briefly heating them with vegetables or pasta, it's easier to ensure that they do not overcook. Ground beef, chicken, and turkey are perfect ingredients to use as the basis for quick, meal-in-a-skillet casseroles.

Fish and quick-cooking shellfish like shrimp and scallops are also terrific candidates for turning into stovetop casseroles. It's easier to keep an eye on fish, especially thin, delicate fillets, when it's cooking gently in a skillet on the stove instead of in a casserole in the oven. Similarly, green vegetables such as sugar snap peas, broccoli, and green beans keep their color better in a briefly simmered stovetop casserole than in an oven-baked dish.

With some meat and vegetable casseroles, you have your choice—you can either simmer them on top of the stove or bake them according to your preference. If the oven is busy because you're baking a cake, for example, you can cook these casseroles on a burner. Moroccan-Style Ratatouille can either cook gently on the stove over low heat or be baked in the oven in a covered dish at a moderate temperature. Rice casseroles that start with uncooked rice, such as Cumin-Scented Lentil and Rice Casserole with Yogurt-Mint Sauce (page 138) or Rice Pilaf with Dried Cranberries and Pecans (page 73), also are good prepared either way. Long-cooking beef casseroles, such as Baked Beef and Green Bean Curry with Cilantro (page 20), offer you the same flexibility.

Since stovetop casseroles aren't hidden in the oven, there is more room for you to add your personal touch while you watch it simmer. Add extra seasonings if you wish, or moisten the dish during cooking with a bit of wine or broth. If you have fresh herbs, stir some in at the last moment to give the casserole added flavor.

# Moroccan-Style Ratatouille

3 tablespoons olive oil

1 large onion, halved and thinly sliced

1 red bell pepper, cut into ½-inch strips

1 green bell pepper, cut into ½-inch strips

12 ounces small zucchini, diced

Salt and freshly ground black pepper

1 pound Japanese eggplant, cut into ½-inch slices, or Italian eggplant, cut into ¾-inch cubes

3 large cloves garlic, chopped

1 jalapeño pepper, seeds removed if desired, and minced

1 teaspoon ground cumin

1 pound ripe tomatoes, peeled, seeded (see page xviii), and chopped, or one 28-ounce can diced tomatoes, drained

¼ cup chopped cilantro or fresh Italian parsley

*F*ood lovers are familiar with the basil-accented southern French version of ratatouille, made of eggplant, zucchini, bell peppers, and tomatoes. In fact, this vegetable casserole is popular in many lands around the Mediterranean, with the seasonings differing from place to place. For this interpretation, inspired by the favorite flavors of North Africa, the vegetables are spiced with cilantro, cumin, and hot peppers. Couscous is the perfect accompaniment.

*Makes 4 servings*

In a large, wide casserole, heat 2 tablespoons of the oil over medium heat. Add the onion and bell peppers and sauté until the onion begins to turn golden, about 5 minutes. Add the zucchini and salt and pepper to taste. Cover and cook 3 minutes. Transfer the vegetables to a bowl.

In the casserole, heat the remaining 1 tablespoon oil over medium heat. Add the eggplant and salt and pepper to taste and sauté, stirring, until the pan is dry, about 2 minutes. Add the garlic, jalapeño pepper, cumin, and tomatoes and bring to a boil. Cover and cook over medium heat 5 minutes.

Return the zucchini-pepper mixture to the casserole and mix gently. Bring to a boil. Cook, uncovered, over medium-high heat, stirring occasionally, until the vegetables are tender, about 5 minutes. Stir in 3 tablespoons of the cilantro. Taste and adjust the seasonings, generously adding pepper if desired. Serve sprinkled with the remaining cilantro.

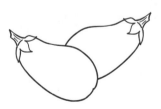

# Hot Orzo with Onions

3 tablespoons olive oil

3 large onions (about 1¹/₂ pounds), halved and cut into thin slices lengthwise

Salt

2 jalapeño peppers, seeded if desired, and minced

1 cup tomato sauce (page 154)

1 cup vegetable (page 160) or chicken stock (page 157)

2 teaspoons dried oregano

Freshly ground black pepper

2 cups boiling water

1 pound orzo or riso (rice-shaped pasta)

3 tablespoons chopped fresh Italian parsley

Cayenne pepper (optional)

*Aromatic, slow-cooked onions give this casserole of rice-shaped pasta a wonderful flavor. Jalapeño peppers provide plenty of punch for most palates, but if you'd like your pasta even hotter, season the finished dish with cayenne pepper. Serve it with grilled chicken or steak or as a vegetarian entrée with a green salad or a light coleslaw. To temper the heat of the chiles, you might also like to serve an accompanying salad of yogurt mixed with diced cucumbers and dill.*

*Makes about 6 servings*

In a heavy Dutch oven, heat the oil over medium heat. Add the onions and salt to taste; sauté until the pan is dry, about 10 minutes. Cover and cook over low heat, stirring often, until tender and beginning to brown, about 15 minutes. Stir in the jalapeño peppers, tomato sauce, stock, oregano, and salt and pepper to taste. Add the boiling water, then stir in the pasta. Cover and cook over low heat just until tender, about 15 minutes. Stir in the parsley. Taste and adjust the seasonings; add cayenne pepper to taste if desired. Serve hot.

# Black-eyed Peas with Rice and Peppers

**One 1-pound package frozen black-eyed peas**

**One 14$^1$/$_2$-ounce can vegetable broth (1$^3$/$_4$ cups)**

**$^1$/$_2$ cup water**

**2 tablespoons vegetable oil**

**1 large onion, chopped**

**1 large red bell pepper, diced**

**1 jalapeño pepper, seeded and chopped**

**1 teaspoon ground cumin**

**1$^1$/$_2$ cups long-grain white rice**

**Salt and freshly ground black pepper**

**1 tablespoon chopped cilantro or fresh Italian parsley (optional)**

*ere is a colorful, healthful rendition of black-eyed peas with rice, a favorite in the South when celebrating the New Year. The casserole gains its lively flavor from sautéed onions, jalapeño and bell peppers, and cumin. I love it as a vegetarian main course, but it's also delicious with roasted chicken.*

*Makes 6 servings*

In a large saucepan, combine the black-eyed peas, broth, and water. Bring to a boil, cover, and cook over medium heat for 25 minutes. Drain the liquid into a measuring cup and add enough water to make 3 cups; reserve.

In a heavy, medium skillet, heat the oil over medium heat. Add the onion and bell pepper and sauté, stirring occasionally, until the onion begins to brown, about 10 minutes. Add the jalapeño pepper and cumin and sauté 30 seconds.

To the pan of black-eyed peas, add the measured liquid and bring to a boil. Add the rice and the salt and pepper to taste and return to a boil. Reduce the heat to low. Add the onion-pepper mixture. Cover and cook, without stirring, until the rice and black-eyed peas are tender, 18 to 20 minutes. Taste and adjust the seasonings. Serve hot, sprinkled with the cilantro or parsley if desired.

# Three-Bean Casserole with Tomatoes and Garlic

**One 10-ounce package frozen lima beans**

**4 ounces green beans, trimmed and broken in half**

**4 ounces wax beans or additional green beans, trimmed and broken in half**

**2 teaspoons olive oil**

**2 large cloves garlic, minced**

**1 green onion, white and green parts chopped**

**One 14$^1$/$_2$-ounce can diced tomatoes, drained**

**$^1$/$_2$ teaspoon dried oregano**

**Salt and freshly ground black pepper**

*T*his casserole of green, yellow, and lima beans is one of the most versatile of dishes and is a favorite of students in my cooking classes. It's not only quick but also low in fat. In addition, it's colorful, delicious, and needs only one pan. Serve it as the center of a vegetarian meal along with rice or crusty sourdough bread, or as an accompaniment for chicken, beef, or lamb.

*Makes 4 servings*

In a large saucepan of boiling water, cook the lima beans 3 minutes. Add the green beans and wax beans and boil until all the beans are tender, about 5 minutes. Drain well.

In the same saucepan, heat the oil over low heat, add the garlic and green onion and sauté 10 seconds. Add the tomatoes and oregano and heat through. Add the beans and season to taste with salt and pepper. Serve hot.

# Skillet Steak with Baby Corn, Mint, and Chiles

**3 to 4 tablespoons vegetable oil**

**1 large onion, halved lengthwise and thinly sliced**

**2 red or green jalapeño peppers, halved lengthwise**

**8 ounces good-quality boneless steak, such as rib eye, trimmed of fat and cut into ¼-inch strips**

**3 large cloves garlic, minced**

**4 green onions, white and light green parts chopped, dark green part cut into 3-inch pieces**

**½ cup beef stock (page 158)**

**2 tablespoons soy sauce**

**1 tablespoon oyster sauce**

**One 5½-ounce can baby corn, drained, halved if long**

**1 cup whole fresh mint leaves**

*C*hiles and mint are a favorite Thai combination, with the mint's freshness acting as a counterpoint to the heat of the peppers. They make a lively flavoring pair for the beef in this casserole. I leave the chiles in large pieces so they can flavor and garnish the dish and can be removed by those who prefer not to eat them. If you wish to reduce their heat, remove the seeds before adding the chiles to the pan. I like to serve this quick entrée over jasmine rice.

*Makes 3 servings*

In a large skillet or wok, heat 1 to 2 tablespoons of the oil over medium heat. Add the onion and jalapeño peppers and sauté, stirring, until the onion browns lightly, about 7 minutes; it may still be a bit crunchy. Transfer to a bowl.

Add 1 tablespoon of the oil to the skillet and heat over high heat. Add the steak and sauté until it changes color, about 1 minute. Add to the onions.

Heat the remaining tablespoon oil in the skillet over medium-low heat. Add the garlic and all of the green onions and sauté 30 seconds. Add the stock, soy sauce, oyster sauce, and baby corn and heat through. Add the steak mixture and mint leaves and toss 30 seconds over low heat. Taste and add more soy sauce if needed.

# Fideos with Turkey, Summer Squash, and Cumin-Tomato Sauce

¹/₄ cup vegetable oil

8 ounces fideos (coiled thin noodles) or vermicelli, broken into 2- to 3-inch pieces

¹/₃ cup minced onion

1 fresh mild green chile (such as California or Anaheim) or Italian frying pepper, or ¹/₂ green bell pepper, chopped

3 large cloves garlic, minced

One 28-ounce can diced tomatoes, drained

1 teaspoon ground cumin

1 teaspoon dried oregano

1¹/₂ cups chicken stock (page 157)

Salt and freshly ground black pepper

2¹/₂ cups shredded cooked chicken or turkey

2 golden or green zucchini or yellow crookneck squash, cut into 1-inch cubes

¹/₄ cup chopped green onion, white and green parts, or cilantro

Hot sauce to taste (optional)

*If your market carries the thin coiled Spanish noodles called fideos, use them in this casserole or substitute vermicelli. For this easy entrée, the pasta is sautéed, then cooks right in the sauce. This technique enables the noodles to absorb more flavor from the sauce and eliminates the need for another pot. The tomato sauce is flavored with a fresh mild chile, but you can use an Italian or a Hungarian pepper or a bell pepper instead. Use golden zucchini when they are available—they add a colorful note to the dish. Use cooked turkey or chicken if you have some on hand, or buy roasted turkey at a deli or supermarket.*

*Makes 3 to 4 servings*

In a large skillet, heat 3 tablespoons of the oil over medium heat. Add the noodles and sauté, stirring constantly and turning over from time to time, until golden, about 6 minutes. With tongs or a slotted spoon, transfer to a bowl. (A few noodles may remain in the pan.)

Add the remaining tablespoon of oil to the skillet and heat over low heat. Add the onion and chile and cook, stirring often, until the onion softens, about 5 minutes. Add the garlic, tomatoes, cumin, and oregano, stir well, and bring to a boil. Add the stock and a pinch of salt and pepper and return to a boil. Add the sautéed noodles and stir. Cover and simmer over low heat 7 minutes. Add the chicken and squash. Cover and simmer, stirring occasionally, until the liquid is absorbed and the pasta is tender, about 5 minutes; if the pan becomes dry, add a few tablespoons water. Add 3 tablespoons of the green onion. Taste and adjust the seasonings; add the hot sauce if desired. Serve sprinkled with the remaining green onion.

# Sweet-and-Sour Apricot Chicken

2 tablespoons vegetable oil

1 large onion, chopped

1¼ pounds boneless, skinless chicken breasts or thighs, cut into 1-inch cubes

1 cup dried apricots, rinsed and quartered

2 tablespoons sugar

3 tablespoons rice vinegar

3 tablespoons ketchup

3 tablespoons soy sauce

¼ cup chicken stock (page 157)

1½ teaspoons cornstarch mixed with 1 tablespoon water

White pepper

*T*his savory, easy-to-prepare chicken casserole cooks with dried apricots and a simple Chinese sweet-and-sour sauce. Use boneless thighs or breasts for this entrée, depending on whether you prefer chicken that is rich or lean. Serve it with steamed rice. Snow peas or sugar snap peas are a great accompaniment.

*Makes 4 servings*

In a heavy, nonstick sauté pan, heat the oil over medium heat. Add the onion and sauté, stirring often, until it begins to turn golden, about 7 minutes. Add the chicken and sauté over medium heat, stirring, 1 minute. Cover and sauté 3 minutes, stirring once or twice. Add the apricots.

In a small bowl, mix the sugar, vinegar, ketchup, soy sauce, and stock. Add to the pan of chicken and mix well. Bring to a simmer. Cover and cook over low heat until the chicken is tender, about 5 minutes; cut into a thick piece to check—the color should no longer be pink.

Pour the cornstarch mixture into the center of the simmering sauce. Quickly stir into the remaining sauce. Heat until bubbling. Season to taste with white pepper. Serve hot.

# Microwave Casseroles

*Halibut with Peppers, Mushrooms, and Soy Sauce*

*Cajun-Spiced Chicken Casserole*

*Black-eyed Peas with Salami and Corn*

*Easy Microwave Chili with Zucchini*

*Sugar Snap Pea and Baby Onion Medley with Water Chestnuts*

*Chickpea and Rice Casserole with Bell Pepper*

*Brown Rice with Broccoli and Garlic*

The microwave has two advantages for making casseroles: First, it cuts cooking time drastically, so you can get a home-cooked meal on the table in minutes. Second, it doesn't heat up the kitchen, a great bonus in hot weather. You can also use the microwave to precook individual ingredients for casseroles, to cook casserole mixtures, and to reheat casseroles that were baked or simmered.

Since fish cooks beautifully in the microwave, casseroles made with fish are a terrific choice for a delicious entrée that's ready in a flash. Before microwaving, top the fish with aromatic vegetables, as in Halibut with Peppers, Mushrooms, and Soy Sauce. Another way to prepare a quick fish entrée is to combine fish with cooked rice or pasta, add herbs and a little oil, and heat the casserole in the microwave.

Bean casseroles are among the most nutritious of main courses and can be one of the fastest. Begin with canned or frozen beans, add tomatoes or other vegetables and spices, and heat the mixture in the microwave. For a heartier casserole, you can add some cooked meat or deli meat, as in Black-eyed Peas with Salami and Corn, or use ground beef, chicken, or turkey to make an effortless bowl of chili (page 128).

For a quick supper I often prepare casseroles of grains or pasta with vegetables. Generally, I have rice or another grain already cooked, since I prepare extra to keep in the refrigerator or freezer for quick meals. I boil or microwave one or two vegetables, mix them with the cooked grain or pasta, and add seasonings. Then I briefly heat the mixture in the microwave. For example, in Brown Rice with Broccoli and Garlic, I microwave the broccoli and mix it with cooked brown rice and sautéed garlic, thyme, and cayenne pepper. If I don't have cooked brown rice, I use the quick-cooking variety and simmer it while the broccoli is cooking. This type of casserole is easy, delicious, and low in fat.

For variety, I might use cauliflower, carrots, zucchini, winter squash, green beans, mushrooms, onions, or combinations of these vegetables. When I don't have fresh vegetables, I use frozen, either single vegetables or mixtures like broccoli, corn, and red peppers. When I have fresh basil, chives, cilantro, or other herbs, I scatter them over the casserole at the last minute to dress it up and add a lovely color, flavor, and fragrance. Occasionally I serve grated Parmesan cheese to sprinkle lightly over each portion.

Since microwaving food in a covered dish keeps it moist, it's easy to use this technique for creating low-fat casseroles. I like to add a touch of oil for flavor, but you can omit it.

*Note: The casseroles in this chapter were tested in an 800-watt microwave oven. If your oven has a lower wattage, the recipes will need a slightly longer cooking time.*

# Halibut with Peppers, Mushrooms, and Soy Sauce

**1¹/₂ pounds halibut fillets, cut into 4 pieces**

**1 tablespoon plus 1 teaspoon soy sauce**

**1 teaspoon grated peeled gingerroot**

**1 large clove garlic, minced**

**2 teaspoons vegetable oil**

**¹/₄ teaspoon hot pepper sauce, or to taste**

**2 red bell peppers, diced**

**6 ounces sliced mushrooms**

**2 tablespoons chopped cilantro**

*Preparing a fish for supper is a snap when you combine it with vegetables for a microwave-cooked casserole. For even speedier preparation, you can use packaged sliced mushrooms. If your family doesn't like cilantro, substitute green onions or chives and sprinkle them on the finished casserole.*

*Makes 4 servings*

In a shallow casserole, arrange the fish in one layer. In a small bowl, mix the soy sauce, gingerroot, garlic, oil, and hot pepper sauce. Brush over the fish. Sprinkle with the peppers, mushrooms, and 1 tablespoon of the cilantro. Cover and microwave on High until the fish can be flaked with a fork, 5 to 8 minutes, checking every minute or so. Serve sprinkled with the remaining cilantro.

# Cajun-Spiced Chicken Casserole

2 teaspoons sweet paprika

1/4 to 1/2 teaspoon cayenne pepper

Salt

1/4 teaspoon freshly ground black or white pepper

1 teaspoon dried oregano

1 teaspoon dried thyme

2 large cloves garlic, minced

1/4 cup olive oil or melted butter

2 cups diced cooked chicken

One 10-ounce package medium or large pasta shells (about 4 cups)

One 1-pound package frozen mixed vegetables

1/4 cup plus 2 tablespoons minced green onions, white and green parts

Hot pepper sauce (optional)

*Turn leftover cooked chicken or beef into this zesty, easy-to-make entrée. Pasta shells and frozen mixed vegetables complete this casserole, which is flavored with fresh garlic, herbs, and plenty of spice. It will wake up anyone's taste buds! I like to serve it with sliced cucumbers as a cool counterpoint to its spiciness.*

*Makes 4 servings*

In a medium bowl, mix the paprika, 1/4 teaspoon of the cayenne, salt to taste, black or white pepper, oregano, and thyme. Add the garlic and 2 tablespoons of the oil and mix well. Add the chicken and stir to coat.

In a large pot of boiling salted water, cook the pasta, uncovered, over high heat, 2 minutes. Add the frozen vegetables, return to a boil, and cook, stirring occasionally, until the pasta is tender but firm to the bite, about 7 minutes. Drain, rinse with cold water, and drain well. Transfer to a bowl and toss with the remaining 2 tablespoons oil. Add the chicken mixture and mix well. Add 1/4 cup of the green onions and mix well. Taste and adjust the seasonings; add the remaining 1/4 teaspoon cayenne if desired or hot sauce to taste. Mix well.

Transfer to a 2 1/2-quart casserole. Cover and microwave on High until the mixture is completely heated through, about 5 minutes; the bottom of the casserole dish should feel hot. Serve sprinkled with the remaining green onions.

# Black-eyed Peas with Salami and Corn

One 10-ounce package
  frozen corn (2 cups)

One 1-pound package
  frozen black-eyed peas
  (2½ cups)

2 large carrots, scraped and
  sliced ⅓ inch thick

½ cup water

1 cup finely diced salami

½ red onion, chopped

½ cup coarsely chopped
  fresh Italian parsley

Salt and freshly ground
  black pepper

*C*arrots, red onion, and lots of parsley add flavor and color to
  this effortless one-dish meal. This dish is a good example of
how a small amount of meat acts as a condiment to flavor a generous quantity of vegetables. Instead of salami, you can add sliced,
cooked sausages. For a quick supper, serve this casserole with a
green salad and country bread. It's also great served over rice. To
save time, chop the vegetables while the black-eyed peas are cooking in the microwave.

*Makes 4 servings*

Remove the corn from the freezer. In a 3-quart casserole, combine the black-eyed peas, carrots, and water. Cover and
microwave on High for 15 minutes. Stir in the salami and
corn. Cover and microwave on High for 3 minutes. Stir, cover,
and microwave until the vegetables are tender, about 2 more
minutes. Drain off most of the liquid unless you are serving
the casserole with rice.

   To the casserole, add the onion and parsley and mix well.
Season to taste with plenty of pepper; season only lightly with
salt since salami is salty. Serve hot.

# Easy Microwave Chili with Zucchini

1 large onion, chopped

1/2 green bell pepper, diced

1 tablespoon olive oil or vegetable oil

12 ounces lean or extra-lean ground beef

4 large cloves garlic, minced

2 tablespoons chili powder

2 tablespoons ground cumin

1 tablespoon dried oregano

1/2 teaspoon hot red pepper flakes, or 1/4 teaspoon cayenne pepper, or to taste

One 14 1/2-ounce can diced tomatoes, with juice

One 15-ounce can pinto beans, drained

Salt and freshly ground black pepper

3 medium zucchini, diced

*S*ome days I prefer chili with meat and no beans, while at other times I opt for beans and no meat. For this chili casserole I use both and add zucchini too. I find that a vegetable cuts the richness of the chili and makes the dish even better. Best of all, with the microwave your chili is ready in a few moments. To save even more time, you can skip most of the vegetable preparation by using 1 cup of packaged diced onions, which are available fresh and frozen, and about 1/2 cup of frozen strips of bell pepper.

Serve the chili from the casserole with hot tortillas, bread, crackers, or corn chips. You might like to put out small bowls of fresh garnishes to sprinkle on top, such as chopped cilantro, sliced green onions, and fresh tomato or tomatillo salsa. Sour cream, grated cheddar cheese, and diced avocado are sometimes served with chili, but since this casserole is already rich, they aren't really necessary.

*Makes 4 servings*

In a 2-quart casserole, combine the onion, bell pepper, and oil. Cover and microwave on High for 3 minutes. Add the beef in small bits, stir well, and add the garlic. Microwave, uncovered, until the beef is no longer pink, about 5 minutes, stirring once or twice. Stir in the chili powder, cumin, oregano, red pepper flakes, tomatoes, beans, and salt and pepper to taste. Cover and microwave until the mixture is hot and bubbling, about 10 minutes, stirring once or twice. Stir in the zucchini. Cover and microwave until tender, 2 to 4 minutes. Let stand, covered, 1 to 2 minutes. Taste and adjust the seasonings.

# Sugar Snap Pea and Baby Onion Medley with Water Chestnuts

**One 10-ounce package frozen pearl onions**

**2 tablespoons water**

**8 ounces sugar snap peas, trimmed**

**One 8-ounce can sliced water chestnuts, drained**

**1 tablespoon finely grated peeled gingerroot**

**1 tablespoon soy sauce**

**1 tablespoon rice wine vinegar**

**1 teaspoon vegetable oil**

**$1/4$ teaspoon sugar**

**Salt and freshly ground black pepper**

This tasty casserole flavored with gingerroot, soy sauce, and rice vinegar is an easy, low-fat alternative to a stir-fry. And no stirring and frying is needed; everything just cooks in a casserole in the microwave.

*Makes 4 servings*

Combine the onions and water in a 2-quart casserole. Cover and microwave on High until warm, about 4 minutes. Add the remaining ingredients except the salt and pepper. Cover and microwave on High until the sugar snap peas are crisp-tender, about 3 minutes. Add salt and pepper to taste. Stir and serve.

# Chickpea and Rice Casserole with Bell Pepper

1 onion, halved and sliced thin

1 red or green bell pepper, cut into ⅓-inch strips

1 teaspoon olive oil

2 cups cooked rice

One 15½-ounce can chickpeas, drained

1 tablespoon chopped cilantro or fresh oregano, or
1 teaspoon dried oregano

½ teaspoon ground cumin

Salt and freshly ground black pepper

Consider this savory, low-fat casserole a basic recipe that can be varied in many ways. Use any canned beans you like, or substitute 1½ to 2 cups cooked dried beans. This casserole is amazingly easy and will come to the rescue on occasions when you need a main course to put on the table right away. Mix the beans with microwave-sautéed onions and peppers, then with cooked rice, cumin, and cilantro. Serve the casserole as a vegetarian main course or as a satisfying side dish for chicken or meat.

*Makes 2 to 3 main-course servings;
4 to 5 side-dish servings*

In a 2-quart casserole, combine the onion, bell pepper, and oil. Microwave, uncovered, on High for 4 minutes, stirring after 2 minutes. Add the remaining ingredients. Cover and microwave until hot, about 2 minutes if rice was already hot or about 5 minutes if rice was cold. Stir lightly with a fork. Taste and adjust the seasonings. Serve hot.

# Brown Rice with Broccoli and Garlic

2 large cloves garlic,
    minced

2 teaspoons olive oil

1¼ pounds broccoli,
    divided into florets

2 tablespoons water

2 cups cooked brown rice

1 teaspoon dried thyme

Salt and freshly ground
    black pepper

Cayenne pepper

For a no-fuss supper in a few minutes, serve this healthful vegetarian entrée composed of a grain and a nutrient-rich crucif-
erous vegetable (from the cabbage family). Even if you serve this
casserole with a light sprinkling of grated Parmesan cheese, it will
still be low in fat. If you like, garnish each plate with ripe cherry
tomatoes.

*Makes 2 to 3 main-course servings;*
*4 to 5 side-dish servings*

In a 9-inch square casserole, combine the garlic and oil. Microwave, uncovered, on High for 1 minute. Add the broccoli and
water. Cover and microwave until the broccoli is crisp-tender,
about 7 minutes. Add the cooked brown rice, thyme, and salt,
black pepper, and cayenne to taste. Stir the mixture lightly with
a fork. Cover and microwave until the casserole is hot, about
4 minutes. Taste and adjust the seasonings. Serve hot.

# Low-Fat Casseroles

*Shrimp, Rice, and Tomatoes Baked with Capers*

*Quick Couscous and Chicken Casserole with
Roasted Peppers and Mint*

*Provençal Chicken with White Beans, Tomatoes, and Thyme*

*Cumin-Scented Lentil and Rice Casserole with Yogurt-Mint Sauce*

*Baked Eggplant Curry with Peas*

*Fusilli and Spiced Onion Casserole*

*Fat-Free Bean Casserole with Zucchini and Sun-Dried Tomatoes*

For healthful entrées, your best bet is to prepare vegetarian casseroles. Whether your casserole is based on beans, rice, or pasta, if you use oil and cheese sparingly, it is sure to be low in fat. And it can still be delicious as long as you use bold seasonings. Be generous with flavorings such as fresh herbs, fresh garlic, gingerroot, and ripe tomatoes, as in Baked Eggplant Curry with Peas.

Fish is another excellent choice for low-fat casseroles because it is naturally lean. If you feel like serving a meaty casserole, choose low-fat meats such as skinless chicken and turkey breasts. When shopping for beef, buy the leaner "select" rather than "choice" or "prime." Always trim the visible fat from all meat and poultry before cooking. Note also that ground meat is available in much leaner versions than it used to be. You'll find ground beef with a fat content as low as 7 percent.

Whether you are preparing a casserole of meat, fish, pasta, or grains, try to include a generous amount of vegetables and a minimal amount of meat. By doing this, you turn meat casseroles into wholesome entrées. You can enjoy the taste of the meat without eating a large portion of it.

If your favorite casserole calls for cheese, use a flavorful type like Parmesan or Pecorino Romano. Because each spoonful packs a punch of taste, you can add much less than you would of milder cheeses like mozzarella or Swiss. Use low-fat or nonfat cottage cheese and sour cream in your casseroles. If you're making white sauce, use low-fat or skim milk.

Substitute olive oil or vegetable oil for butter in order to use less saturated fat. To reduce the amount of fat needed for sautéing, use nonstick pans. When sautéing vegetables such as onions, peppers, mushrooms, zucchini, or eggplant, begin with a tiny amount of oil. Once the vegetable has absorbed the oil and the pan appears dry, add a few tablespoons of vegetable or chicken stock or water and cover the pan. The vegetables will have an appealing sautéed taste but will have been cooked in a small amount of oil.

To complement your low-fat casseroles, keep the rest of the menu nutritious too. Begin every meal with a big salad. Take advantage of the variety of cleaned, ready-to-eat salad greens available and top them with ripe tomatoes, red bell peppers, sliced fresh mushrooms, thin cucumber slices, bean sprouts, fresh herbs, chopped green onions, or capers. Dress the salad lightly, using a minimal amount of oil. If you like, you can use just balsamic vinegar or bottled fat-free dressing. Keep a good selection of fruits of the season in your fruit bowl and serve them often as enticing snacks and nourishing desserts.

In addition to the recipes in this chapter, you will find many examples of low-fat casseroles throughout the book, both for main courses and side dishes.

# Shrimp, Rice, and Tomatoes Baked with Capers

6 cups water

Salt

1¹/₃ cups long-grain rice

3 tablespoons olive oil

1¹/₄ pounds medium
shrimp, shelled

1¹/₂ cups sliced green
onions, white and
green parts

One 14¹/₂-ounce can diced
tomatoes, drained

2 tablespoons capers,
drained

1 teaspoon dried oregano

Freshly ground black
pepper

*I*ndian and Persian cuisines boast many casseroles made of rice
dotted with tasty bits of chicken or meat. These casseroles
vaguely inspired this one, but its tomatoes, capers, and generous
amount of green onion give it a Mediterranean soul. This delicious,
colorful dish makes an elegant main course that's easy to prepare
and is low in fat. I like to serve it with snow peas or green beans.

*Makes 4 to 5 servings*

Preheat the oven to 375°F. In a large saucepan, bring the water
to a boil with a pinch of salt. Add the rice and boil, uncovered,
until just tender, 12 to 14 minutes. Drain, rinse with cold
water, and drain well. Transfer to a large bowl.

In a large skillet, heat 2 tablespoons of the oil over medium heat. Add the shrimp and sauté, stirring, 1 minute. Add
the green onions and sauté until the shrimp turn pink, 1 to
2 more minutes. Transfer to the bowl of rice. Add the tomatoes, capers, oregano, and salt and pepper to taste. Mix lightly.

Transfer the mixture to an oiled 2-quart casserole. Drizzle
the remaining tablespoon oil over the top. Cover and bake
30 minutes, or until the casserole is hot.

# Quick Couscous and Chicken Casserole with Roasted Peppers and Mint

Two 14½-ounce cans chicken broth

2 tablespoons extra virgin olive oil

1 cup frozen corn

1 cup frozen peas

One 10-ounce package couscous

2 cups finely diced cooked chicken

½ cup diced roasted peppers (homemade, see page xvii, or from a jar)

¼ cup chopped fresh mint

¼ cup chopped green onions, white and green parts

Salt and freshly ground black pepper

Cayenne pepper

*Mint gives this casserole a refreshing quality, almost like a salad. In fact, in summer you can serve the casserole cold—just let the couscous cool before adding the chicken, omit the baking step, and if you like, flavor the mixture with a squeeze of lemon or lime juice. Serve the casserole with a salad of ripe tomatoes or a green salad.*

*Makes 4 servings*

Preheat the oven to 350°F. In a medium saucepan, bring the broth and 1 tablespoon of the oil to a boil. Add the corn and peas and return to a boil. Stir in the couscous. Remove from the heat, cover, and let stand 5 minutes. Add the chicken, peppers, mint, and green onions and toss well. Season to taste with salt, black pepper, and cayenne.

Transfer the couscous mixture to a lightly oiled 2-quart baking dish. Sprinkle with the remaining oil. Cover and bake for 20 minutes, or until hot.

# Provençal Chicken with White Beans, Tomatoes, and Thyme

1½ cups dried white beans, such as great Northern

5 cups cold water

1 sprig fresh thyme (optional)

2 bay leaves

2 tablespoons olive oil

1 large onion, chopped

2 large cloves garlic, chopped

1½ pounds ripe tomatoes, peeled, seeded (see page xviii), and chopped, or one 28-ounce can plus one 14½-ounce can tomatoes, drained and chopped

Salt and freshly ground black pepper

1 tablespoon chopped fresh thyme, or 1 teaspoon dried

2½ pounds chicken pieces, skin removed

*W*hen I studied cooking in Paris, I learned that beans and chicken make a wonderful casserole because the beans gain a rich flavor from baking with the chicken. The tomatoes, olive oil, and thyme give this dish a southern French accent. To save time, you can substitute two 16-ounce cans white beans for the dried beans; simply drain and add to the casserole dish. Serve this casserole with country bread and a salad of baby greens.

*Makes 4 servings*

Sort the beans, discarding any broken ones and any stones. In a large bowl, soak the beans in the cold water overnight. Or cover the beans with the water in a large saucepan, boil 2 minutes, remove from the heat, and let stand for 1 hour.

Rinse and drain the beans and put them in a large saucepan. Add enough water to cover by at least 2 inches. Add the thyme sprig and 1 bay leaf. Cover and bring to a boil over medium heat. Reduce the heat to low and simmer until just tender, about 1½ hours, adding hot water if needed so that the beans remain covered. Keep the beans in their cooking liquid.

Preheat the oven to 375°F. In a large skillet, heat the oil over medium-low heat. Add the onion and cook until softened, about 7 minutes. Stir in the garlic, tomatoes, remaining bay leaf, and a little salt and pepper to taste. Cook over medium heat, stirring often, until thick, about 15 minutes. Discard the bay leaf. Add the chopped thyme and taste for seasonings.

Remove the thyme sprig and bay leaf from the beans. With a slotted spoon, gently transfer the beans to a shallow 2-quart baking dish, reserving a few tablespoons of the bean liquid. Gently mix all but ¼ cup sauce into the beans and taste for seasonings. Arrange the chicken pieces on top of the beans. Spoon the reserved sauce over the chicken and smooth it out. Cover and bake 25 minutes. Add 1 to 2 tablespoons bean liquid if the mixture looks dry. Cover and bake 25 minutes more, or until the chicken is tender.

# Cumin-Scented Lentil and Rice Casserole with Yogurt-Mint Sauce

1 cup lentils

2 cups water

2 tablespoons olive oil

2 large onions, chopped

1 teaspoon ground cumin

$^1/_4$ teaspoon hot red pepper flakes, or to taste

Salt and freshly ground black pepper

$1^1/_2$ cups long-grain white rice

## Yogurt-Mint Sauce

1 cup plain nonfat yogurt

1 tablespoon chopped fresh mint, or 1 teaspoon dried

1 small clove garlic, finely minced

Salt

Cayenne pepper

*During the years that I lived in Israel, I often enjoyed a Lebanese rice and lentil specialty called* majadrah. *This casserole is based on that dish but is lower in fat, is more generously spiced, and is baked in the oven, so the rice cooks gently and absorbs the flavor of the sautéed onions. Make it with the common brown lentils found at the supermarket. When accompanied by its refreshing yogurt-mint sauce, this casserole makes a nourishing vegetarian main course. Serve it with a colorful chopped salad of tomatoes, cucumbers, and parsley. If you omit the yogurt sauce, the casserole is a terrific partner for grilled chicken.*

*Makes 4 to 5 servings*

Preheat the oven to 350°F. In a medium saucepan, combine the lentils and water. Bring to a boil. Cover and cook over medium heat until the lentils are just tender, about 20 minutes. Drain the liquid into a measuring cup and add enough water to make 3 cups; reserve. Transfer the lentils to a 2-quart casserole.

In a heavy, large skillet, heat the oil over medium heat. Add the onions and sauté, stirring often, until they are well browned, about 10 minutes. Add the cumin and red pepper flakes and sauté 1 minute.

To casserole, add the onion mixture and salt and pepper to taste. Add the measured liquid and rice. Cover and bake 30 to 40 minutes, or until the rice is tender.

Meanwhile, make the sauce. In a small bowl, mix the yogurt, mint, and garlic. Season to taste with salt and cayenne pepper.

Serve the casserole hot, accompanied by the cool sauce.

# Baked Eggplant Curry with Peas

2 tablespoons olive oil

1 large onion, chopped

6 large cloves garlic, minced

1 jalapeño pepper, seeded and minced

1 tablespoon minced peeled gingerroot

2 teaspoons ground coriander

1½ teaspoons ground cumin

½ teaspoon ground turmeric

1¾ pounds Japanese or Italian eggplants, unpeeled, cut into 1-inch cubes

Salt

1 pound ripe tomatoes, peeled, seeded (see page xviii), and coarsely chopped, or one 28-ounce can tomatoes, drained and chopped

1 tablespoon tomato paste mixed with 1 tablespoon water

1½ cups frozen peas, thawed

3 tablespoons chopped cilantro

Cayenne pepper (optional)

*Eggplant does not need to be fried to taste good. If you want proof, bake it in an aromatic tomato sauce flavored with fresh ginger, garlic, ground coriander, and cilantro. Serve this savory dish as a vegetarian entrée with basmati rice or as an accompaniment for roasted turkey or chicken or grilled steaks.*

*Makes 4 servings*

Preheat the oven to 375°F. In a heavy, wide Dutch oven, heat the oil over medium-low heat. Add the onion and cook until soft but not brown, about 5 minutes. Add the garlic, jalapeño pepper, gingerroot, coriander, cumin, and turmeric. Cook the mixture, stirring, 1 minute. Add the eggplant and salt to taste and mix over low heat until the eggplant is coated with the spices. Add the tomatoes and bring to a boil. Stir in the tomato paste mixture.

Cover and bake 40 minutes. Add the peas and 2 tablespoons of the cilantro. Cover and bake 10 minutes, or until the eggplant and peas are very tender. Taste and adjust the seasonings, adding the cayenne if desired. Serve hot, sprinkled with the remaining cilantro.

# Fusilli and Spiced Onion Casserole

3 tablespoons vegetable oil

1½ pounds onions, halved and thinly sliced

¼ teaspoon hot red pepper flakes, or to taste

Salt and freshly ground black pepper

1 teaspoon ground coriander

¾ teaspoon dried oregano

1 teaspoon sweet paprika, plus extra for garnish

8 ounces fusilli, rotini, or other spiral-shaped pasta (about 3 to 3½ cups)

Cayenne pepper (optional)

1½ tablespoons unseasoned bread crumbs

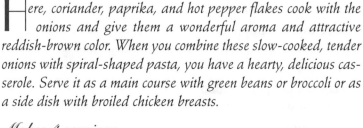

*Here, coriander, paprika, and hot pepper flakes cook with the onions and give them a wonderful aroma and attractive reddish-brown color. When you combine these slow-cooked, tender onions with spiral-shaped pasta, you have a hearty, delicious casserole. Serve it as a main course with green beans or broccoli or as a side dish with broiled chicken breasts.*

*Makes 4 servings*

In a large nonstick sauté pan, heat 2 tablespoons of the oil over medium heat. Add the onions and sauté, stirring often, until the pan is dry, about 5 minutes. Add the red pepper flakes, salt and pepper to taste, coriander, and oregano. Cover and cook over low heat, stirring often, until tender, 10 to 15 minutes; add 1 to 2 tablespoons water if the pan becomes dry. Increase the heat to medium-high, add the teaspoon of paprika, and sauté, stirring, until the onions lightly brown, about 2 minutes. Transfer to a large bowl.

In a large pot of boiling salted water, cook the pasta, uncovered, over high heat until tender but firm to the bite, about 7 minutes. Drain, rinse with cold water, and drain well. Transfer to a large bowl. Add the onion mixture and mix very well. Taste and adjust the seasonings; add the cayenne if desired.

Preheat the oven to 350°F. Transfer the pasta mixture to a lightly oiled 2-quart casserole. Sprinkle with the bread crumbs, drizzle with the remaining 1 tablespoon oil, and top with extra paprika. Bake, uncovered, 30 minutes, or until the top browns lightly.

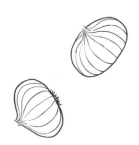

# Fat-Free Bean Casserole with Zucchini and Sun-Dried Tomatoes

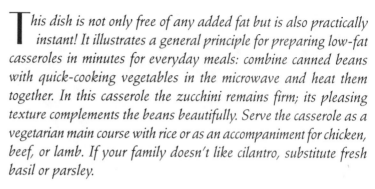

**8 dry-packed sun-dried tomatoes**

**One 15-ounce can pinto beans, drained**

**2 tablespoons dried onion flakes**

**2 medium zucchini (about 8 ounces), cut into ¹/₂-inch cubes**

**Salt and freshly ground black pepper**

**¹/₄ cup coarsely chopped cilantro**

**Hot pepper sauce for serving**

This dish is not only free of any added fat but is also practically instant! It illustrates a general principle for preparing low-fat casseroles in minutes for everyday meals: combine canned beans with quick-cooking vegetables in the microwave and heat them together. In this casserole the zucchini remains firm; its pleasing texture complements the beans beautifully. Serve the casserole as a vegetarian main course with rice or as an accompaniment for chicken, beef, or lamb. If your family doesn't like cilantro, substitute fresh basil or parsley.

*Makes 2 main-course servings;*
*3 to 4 side-dish servings*

In a small bowl, cover the dried tomatoes with boiling water and let stand 1 minute. Remove the tomatoes from the soaking water, reserving the water, and cut each in half.

In a 1¹/₂-quart casserole, combine the beans, tomatoes, dried onion, zucchini, and salt and pepper to taste. Add 2 tablespoons of the tomato soaking water. Cover and microwave on High until hot, about 3 minutes. Stir in the cilantro, cover, and let stand 1 minute. Pass the hot sauce at the table.

# Dessert Casseroles

*Lemon-Scented Noodle and Cottage Cheese Kugel*

*Apple-Apricot Noodle Pudding with Cinnamon and Ginger*

*Noodle Pudding with Pecans and Orange*

*Rice Pudding with Pumpkin and Spice*

*Bread Pudding with Pears and Cranberries*

*Warm Nectarine Flan with Grand Marnier*

*Matzo Kugel with Pears and Strawberry Sauce*

For me, the quintessential dessert casserole is the sweet noodle kugel. This type of noodle pudding is a specialty of eastern European and Jewish cooking. It's a treat I grew up with and enjoyed every week. Traditionally, noodle kugels are made of egg noodles mixed with sugar, eggs, and melted butter or margarine. Customary flavorings are cinnamon, lemon and orange rind, apples, dried fruit, and nuts. For a more lavish dessert, you can stir in sour cream and cottage cheese, as in Lemon-Scented Noodle and Cottage Cheese Kugel.

These sweet casseroles make terrific desserts, but they have other roles. They are served as satisfying main courses for brunch or supper and are especially popular with children. Like main-course casseroles, many dessert casseroles can be made ahead and are easy to serve directly from the baking dish.

Bread puddings and rice puddings are other beloved casserole desserts that are surprisingly easy to make. You can accent them with vanilla, a liqueur, or any of the flavorings that are used for noodle puddings, such as orange rind, lemon, or cinnamon. When you want lighter fare, it's hard to find a more delicious finale to a meal than a casserole of fresh fruit baked with a custard topping, such as Warm Nectarine Flan with Grand Marnier.

Dessert casseroles have a warm, Old World appeal. But the flavors don't need to be old-fashioned. Try combinations that are a bit different from your usual standbys. For example, flavor your next rice pudding with cooked pumpkin and pumpkin pie spices. Or add fresh pears, dried cranberries, and pear brandy to bread pudding for a new twist on a familiar sweet.

# Lemon-Scented Noodle and Cottage Cheese Kugel

1/4 cup butter

8 ounces wide egg noodles

1 cup creamy cottage cheese

1 1/2 cups sour cream, plus extra for serving

4 large eggs, separated

1/4 cup plus 1 tablespoon sugar

1 1/2 teaspoons grated lemon zest

1 tablespoon strained lemon juice

*This is a luxurious casserole, perfect for a winter dessert or for brunch. If you wish to make it leaner, use nonfat cottage cheese and sour cream and omit the egg yolks and half of the butter (the melted portion).*

*Makes 4 to 6 servings*

Preheat the oven to 350°F. Butter a deep 8- to 10-cup baking dish. Melt 2 tablespoons of the butter.

In a large pot of boiling salted water, cook the noodles, uncovered, over high heat, stirring occasionally, until tender but firm to the bite, about 5 minutes. Drain, rinse with cold water, and drain well. Transfer to a large bowl. Toss with the melted butter. Stir in the cottage cheese, sour cream, egg yolks, 1/4 cup of the sugar, the lemon zest, and lemon juice.

In a large bowl, beat the egg whites until soft peaks form. Add the remaining tablespoon of sugar and continue beating until stiff and glossy, about 30 seconds. Gently fold 1/4 of the whites into the noodle mixture; fold in the remaining whites.

Transfer the noodle mixture to the baking dish. Dot with the remaining 2 tablespoons butter. Bake about 50 minutes, or until puffed and golden brown. Serve hot or warm. If desired, serve with additional sour cream.

# Apple-Apricot Noodle Pudding with Cinnamon and Ginger

14 ounces medium egg
noodles

$^1/_4$ cup plus 2 tablespoons
butter or margarine

3 Golden Delicious apples
(about 1$^1/_2$ pounds),
peeled, halved, cored,
and sliced

1 teaspoon ground ginger

$^1/_4$ cup plus 2 tablespoons
sugar

1 teaspoon ground
cinnamon

$^1/_2$ cup blanched almonds,
chopped

$^1/_2$ cup diced dried apricots

4 large eggs, separated

This irresistible egg noodle pudding is studded with almonds, dried apricots, and butter-sautéed apples. For a lovely presentation, top each serving with a dollop of sour cream and accompany it with a few apple slices, either fresh or sautéed.

*Makes 8 servings*

Preheat the oven to 350°F. Grease a 13 × 9-inch baking dish. In a large pot of boiling salted water, cook the noodles until barely tender, about 5 minutes. Drain, rinse with cold water, and drain well. Transfer to a large bowl.

In a large skillet, heat 2 tablespoons of the butter over medium heat. Add half of the apples and sauté 5 minutes, turning once. Remove with a slotted spoon. Add the rest of the apples to the skillet and sauté. Return all the apples to the skillet. Sprinkle with the ginger, 2 tablespoons of the sugar, and $^1/_2$ teaspoon of the cinnamon and sauté 1 minute, tossing the apples to coat. Transfer to a bowl.

Add the remaining $^1/_4$ cup butter to the skillet and melt over low heat. Add 3 tablespoons of the melted butter to the noodles and mix well. Stir in the almonds and apricots.

In a large bowl, whip the egg whites to soft peaks. Beat in the remaining $^1/_4$ cup sugar and whip until the whites are stiff but not dry. Stir the egg yolks into the noodles. Stir in $^1/_4$ of the whipped whites. Fold in the remaining whites.

Spread half of the noodle mixture in the baking dish. Top with the sautéed apples in an even layer. Top with the remaining noodle mixture and spread gently to cover the apples. Sprinkle with the remaining $^1/_2$ teaspoon cinnamon and drizzle with the remaining 1 tablespoon melted butter. Cover the dish and bake 30 minutes. Uncover and bake 15 to 20 minutes, or until set. Serve hot.

# Noodle Pudding with Pecans and Orange

1/4 cup golden raisins

2 tablespoons Grand Marnier or orange juice

2 1/2 cups milk

4 ounces very fine noodles, such as soup noodles (about 2 cups)

Pinch of salt

2 teaspoons finely grated orange zest

1/4 cup plus 2 tablespoons sugar, plus extra sugar to coat baking dish

1/3 cup pecans, coarsely chopped

4 large eggs, separated

*Cooking noodles in milk is a technique I learned in France for making desserts. The noodles contribute a wonderful creamy texture to this sweet casserole, and raisins macerated in Grand Marnier give it zip. To make this dessert festive, you might like to garnish each plate with a few orange segments and top the pudding with a spoonful of softly whipped cream.*

*Makes 4 to 5 servings*

In a jar with a tight-fitting lid, combine the raisins and Grand Marnier. Cover and shake to blend. Let stand about 1 hour.

Preheat the oven to 400°F. In a heavy, medium saucepan, bring the milk to a boil. Add the noodles and salt. Cook over low heat, stirring often with a fork to keep the noodles separate, until the noodles are soft and absorb most of the milk, about 20 minutes. Stir in the orange zest and 1/4 cup of the sugar. Transfer the mixture to a large bowl.

Butter a 6- to 7-cup soufflé dish or deep baking dish and coat the sides lightly with sugar.

Add the pecans to the noodle mixture. Add the raisins with their liquid and the egg yolks and mix well.

In a large bowl, beat the egg whites to soft peaks. Beat in the remaining 2 tablespoons sugar. Whip until the whites are stiff and shiny but not dry, about 30 seconds. In 2 batches, fold the whites into the noodle mixture.

Transfer to the soufflé dish. Bake 28 minutes, or until slightly puffed and firm on top. Serve immediately.

# Rice Pudding with Pumpkin and Spice

2 quarts water

1 cup Arborio or other
short-grain rice

4 cups milk

1 vanilla bean, split

Pinch of salt

$1/3$ cup sugar

One 15-ounce can
pumpkin

1 teaspoon ground
cinnamon, plus extra
for garnish (optional)

$1/2$ teaspoon ground ginger

$1/4$ teaspoon ground
nutmeg

$1/4$ cup raisins

2 tablespoons butter, cut
into small pieces

*I*f rice pudding and pumpkin pie are among your favorite desserts, here's a little bit of both. Half of the pudding is left plain while the other half is mixed with pumpkin, and then the two mixtures are layered. For a practically fat-free dessert, you can use nonfat milk and omit the butter.*

*Makes 4 to 6 servings*

In a heavy, large saucepan, bring the water to a boil and add the rice. Boil, uncovered, 7 minutes; drain well.

Preheat the oven to 350°F. In the same saucepan, bring the milk to a boil over medium-high heat, stirring occasionally. Add the vanilla bean, rice, and salt. Cook, uncovered, over medium-low heat, stirring often, until the rice is very soft and absorbs most of the milk, 15 to 18 minutes. Remove from the heat, remove the vanilla bean, and stir in the sugar.

In a large bowl, mix the pumpkin with half (2 cups) of the rice pudding. Add the cinnamon, ginger, and nutmeg. Spoon the pumpkin rice pudding into a buttered 2-quart baking dish. Mix the raisins into the white rice mixture. Spoon it over the pumpkin mixture. Dot with the butter. Bake, uncovered, 30 minutes, or until firm. Serve warm, sprinkled with cinnamon if desired.

# Bread Pudding with Pears and Cranberries

**4 ounces day-old good-quality egg bread or white bread**

**1¹⁄₄ cups milk**

**¹⁄₄ cup plus 2 tablespoons sugar**

**2 large eggs, separated**

**1¹⁄₂ teaspoons ground cinnamon**

**2 tablespoons pear brandy**

**1 pound ripe but firm pears, peeled, cored, and thinly sliced**

**¹⁄₄ cup dried cranberries**

**2 tablespoons butter, cut into small pieces**

*I*n recent years bread pudding has enjoyed renewed popularity on restaurant menus. It's an easy dessert to make at home and is especially good when flavored with fresh pears, pear liqueur, and colorful dried cranberries. To make the pudding, use any white bread you like; my favorite is challah, or egg bread.

*Makes 4 servings*

Preheat the oven to 400°F. Generously butter a 5-cup baking dish. Remove the crusts from the bread and cut into cubes. Bring the milk to a simmer. Place the bread in a large bowl and pour the hot milk over it. Let stand several minutes so the bread softens.

Mash the bread with a fork. Add ¹⁄₄ cup of the sugar, the egg yolks, 1 teaspoon of the cinnamon, and the brandy and mix well. Add the pears and cranberries and mix to distribute evenly.

In a medium bowl, whip the egg whites until almost stiff. Gradually beat in the remaining 2 tablespoons sugar and beat until stiff and shiny, 15 seconds more. In 2 batches, gently fold the whites into the bread mixture.

Transfer the mixture to the baking dish. Sprinkle with the remaining ¹⁄₂ teaspoon cinnamon and scatter the butter pieces on top. Bake 40 to 50 minutes, or until a thin knife inserted into the center of the pudding comes out dry. Serve hot or warm from the baking dish.

# Warm Nectarine Flan with Grand Marnier

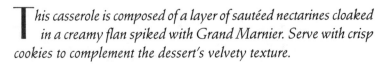

- **3 tablespoons unsalted butter**
- **4 medium nectarines, pitted and thinly sliced**
- **¼ cup plus 2 tablespoons sugar**
- **3 tablespoons Grand Marnier**
- **1½ cups milk**
- **2 large eggs**
- **2 large egg yolks**

*T*his casserole is composed of a layer of sautéed nectarines cloaked in a creamy flan spiked with Grand Marnier. Serve with crisp cookies to complement the dessert's velvety texture.

*Makes 4 servings*

In a large skillet, melt the butter over medium-high heat. Add the nectarine slices and sauté, turning them over occasionally, until light golden, about 2 minutes. Sprinkle with 2 tablespoons of the sugar and continue to sauté over high heat until the sugar caramelizes lightly. Remove from the heat and add 1 tablespoon of the Grand Marnier, turning to coat.

Preheat the oven to 350°F. Generously butter four ⅔- to 1-cup ramekins. Spoon the nectarine mixture into the ramekins. Bring the milk to a boil. Remove from the heat and cool.

In a large bowl, whisk the eggs and egg yolks lightly. Add the remaining ¼ cup sugar and whisk just to blend. Gradually add about 1 cup of the milk in a thin stream, stirring constantly with a whisk. Using a wooden spoon, gradually stir in the remaining milk. Stir in the remaining 2 tablespoons Grand Marnier. Pour into a measuring cup. Skim the foam from the surface of the mixture.

Set the ramekins in a roasting pan or large shallow baking dish. Pour the custard mixture into the ramekins over the nectarine mixture, dividing it evenly among them. Place the pan with the ramekins in the oven. Add enough very hot water to the large pan to come halfway up the sides of the ramekins. Set a sheet of foil on top to cover the ramekins. Bake about 28 minutes, or until a cake tester or point of a small, thin-bladed knife inserted gently in the center of each flan comes out clean. (During baking, if the water in the pan comes close to a boil, add a few tablespoons cold water.)

Carefully remove the ramekins from the water bath. Let cool on a rack until warm or room temperature. Serve warm or cold in the ramekins.

# Matzo Kugel with Pears and Strawberry Sauce

4 matzos

4 large eggs, separated

$1/2$ teaspoon ground cinnamon

$1/4$ cup plus 1 tablespoon sugar

$1/4$ cup butter or margarine, melted and cooled

$1/4$ cup chopped walnuts

3 large ripe pears, peeled, cored, and very thinly sliced

## Strawberry Sauce

4 cups fresh or thawed frozen strawberries

3 to 6 tablespoons powdered sugar, or more to taste, depending on the sweetness of the strawberries, sifted

A few drops fresh lemon juice (optional)

Matzo is a flat, crackerlike bread used for the Jewish holiday of Passover and found with the kosher products in the supermarket. One of the most delicious dishes you can make from matzo is a sweet pudding like this one, studded with fresh pears and delicately flavored with cinnamon and walnuts.

*Makes about 8 servings*

Preheat the oven to 350°F. Grease a deep 7- to 8-cup baking dish. Break the matzos into small pieces and put in a bowl. Cover with boiling water and let stand for 2 minutes. Drain and squeeze out as much water as possible.

In a large bowl, beat the egg yolks with the cinnamon and 3 tablespoons of the sugar until lightened in color. Stir in the matzos, melted butter, walnuts, and pears.

In a large bowl, beat the egg whites until just stiff. Add the remaining 2 tablespoons sugar and beat until glossy, about 30 seconds. Gently fold the egg whites into the matzo mixture. Spoon the mixture into the greased dish. Bake about 40 minutes, or until browned and firm.

Meanwhile, prepare the sauce. In a food processor or blender, puree the strawberries (drained of any juices) until very smooth. Transfer to a bowl and whisk in 3 tablespoons of the powdered sugar. Taste and add more sugar if desired. Add lemon juice if using. Refrigerate until ready to use.

Serve the casserole hot or warm, with cold strawberry sauce on the side.

# Sauces, Dressings, and Stocks

*Quick Tomato Sauce*

*Variation: Tomato-Tarragon Sauce*

*Fresh Herb Vinaigrette*

*Jalapeño-Tomato Salsa*

*Chicken Stock*

*Beef Stock*

*Fish Stock*

*Vegetable Stock*

Casseroles are complete dishes in themselves and rarely need sauces to accompany them. Still, here are a few ideas for when you would like to add an extra touch. Some recipes, like Quick Tomato Sauce and Jalapeño-Tomato Salsa, are useful ingredients to add to casseroles as well as to serve with them.

# Quick Tomato Sauce

**2 large sprigs fresh thyme, or ¹/₂ teaspoon dried**

**1 bay leaf**

**2 tablespoons olive oil or vegetable oil**

**¹/₂ cup minced onion (optional)**

**2 medium cloves garlic, minced**

**2 pounds ripe tomatoes, preferably plum tomatoes, peeled, seeded (see page xviii), and finely chopped, or two 28-ounce cans tomatoes, drained well and chopped**

**Salt and freshly ground black pepper**

Use very ripe plum tomatoes for the best, freshest flavor. If they are not available, prepare the sauce with canned tomatoes. Keep this tomato sauce on hand in your freezer so you can mix it with pasta and vegetables and prepare a casserole with practically no effort.

*Makes about 2 cups*

If using fresh thyme sprigs, tie them and the bay leaf together with kitchen string. In a heavy, large sauté pan or skillet, heat the oil over medium-low heat. Add the onion if using and cook, stirring, until very soft but not browned, about 10 minutes. Add the garlic and cook 30 seconds. Add the tomatoes, thyme bundle (or dried thyme and bay leaf), and salt and pepper to taste and bring to a boil. Cook, uncovered, over medium-high heat, stirring often, 10 minutes. Reduce the heat to medium and cook until the tomatoes are very soft and the sauce is fairly thick, about 5 more minutes. Discard the bay leaf and fresh thyme sprigs. Taste and adjust the seasonings.

## Variation

### Tomato-Tarragon Sauce

*Stir 3 to 4 tablespoons chopped fresh tarragon into the finished sauce.*

# Fresh Herb Vinaigrette

3 tablespoons herb vinegar,
such as tarragon or
mixed herb

1/2 teaspoon Dijon mustard

1/2 small shallot, minced

Salt and freshly ground
black pepper

About 1/2 cup vegetable oil
or olive oil

3 to 4 teaspoons chopped
fresh Italian parsley,
chives, basil, or tarragon

*This classic sauce is great with Seafood Terrine (page 88).*

*Makes about 1/2 cup*

In a small bowl, whisk the vinegar with the mustard, shallot, and salt and pepper to taste. Whisk in the oil. Taste and adjust the seasonings. Just before using, whisk again and add the fresh herbs.

# Jalapeño-Tomato Salsa

1 pound ripe tomatoes, chopped

2 jalapeño peppers, seeds removed if desired, and minced

$1/2$ cup chopped cilantro

2 large green onions, white and green parts, chopped

$1/4$ teaspoon salt, or to taste

2 to 3 tablespoons water (optional)

*F*resh salsa is very easy to make at home and can taste much better than the commercial varieties. Put a bowl of this salsa on the table to add a kick to chicken, meat, or vegetarian casseroles. Remove the seeds from the jalapeño peppers if you don't want the salsa to be very hot. This salsa will keep for 2 days in the refrigerator.

*Makes about 3 cups*

In a medium bowl, combine the tomatoes, jalapeño peppers, cilantro, and green onions. Add the salt. Add the water if the mixture is dry; it should have the texture of a chunky sauce. Serve at room temperature.

# Chicken Stock

**3 pounds whole chicken, chicken parts, or mixture of wings, backs, necks, and giblets (except livers)**

**2 onions, quartered**

**2 carrots, quartered**

**About 4 quarts water**

**2 bay leaves**

**12 stems parsley (optional)**

**2 sprigs fresh thyme, or 1/2 teaspoon dried**

You can use canned chicken broth to prepare casseroles, but when you have homemade chicken stock, the flavor will be superior. I find it convenient to keep stock in the freezer in 2-cup portions.

*Makes about 2 1/2 quarts*

In a stockpot or other large pot, combine the chicken, onions, and carrots. Add enough water to cover the ingredients (about 4 quarts). Bring to a boil, skimming off the froth. Add the bay leaves, parsley, and thyme.

Reduce the heat to low, so that the stock bubbles very gently. Partially cover and cook, skimming off foam and fat occasionally, 2 to 3 hours. Strain the stock into large bowls and cool to lukewarm. Refrigerate until cold and lift solidified fat off the top.

# Beef Stock

4 pounds meaty beef soup
    bones

2 onions, rinsed but not
    peeled, root end cut off,
    quartered

2 carrots, scrubbed but not
    scraped, quartered
    crosswise

2 ribs celery, cut into
    3-inch pieces

3 large cloves garlic,
    unpeeled

About 4 quarts water

2 sprigs fresh thyme, or
    ¹/₂ teaspoon dried

2 bay leaves

12 stems parsley (optional)

*C*asseroles of meat, rice, and pasta benefit from the meaty flavor of this stock. Its cooking time is long, but making it is a
pleasant activity on a cold winter day.

*Makes 1 ¹/₂ to 2 quarts*

Preheat the oven to 450°F. In a large roasting pan, roast the
beef bones, turning them over once, 30 minutes. Add the onions and carrots and roast about 30 minutes, or until browned.

With a slotted metal spoon, transfer the bones and vegetables to a stockpot or other large pot. Add the celery, garlic,
and enough water to cover the ingredients (about 4 quarts).
Bring to a boil, skimming off the froth. Add the thyme, bay
leaves, and parsley. Partially cover and cook over very low heat,
so that stock bubbles very gently, 5 to 6 hours. Skim off foam
and fat occasionally. During the first 2 hours, if necessary, add
hot water to keep the ingredients covered.

Strain the stock into large bowls. Cool the stock, refrigerate until cold, and lift solidified fat off the top.

# Fish Stock

2 pounds fish bones, tails, and heads, or 1½ pounds fish pieces for chowder

1 tablespoon butter or vegetable oil

1 medium onion, halved and thinly sliced

2 quarts water

2 sprigs fresh thyme, or ½ teaspoon dried

1 bay leaf

12 stems parsley

*F*ish stock needs only 20 minutes of simmering. Since prepared fish stock is not widely available at supermarkets, it's a good idea to make it at home. It's a fantastic flavor booster for seafood casseroles.

*Makes about 1½ quarts*

Rinse the fish bones under cold running water for 5 minutes.

In a stockpot or large saucepan, melt the butter over low heat. Add the onion and cook, stirring often, until softened, about 7 minutes. Add the fish bones or fish pieces and the water. Bring to a boil, skimming off any froth. Add the thyme, bay leaf, and parsley. Simmer, uncovered, over medium-low heat, skimming occasionally, 20 minutes.

Strain through a fine strainer into a large bowl. Cool to lukewarm. Refrigerate or freeze.

# Vegetable Stock

2 large onions, diced

2 large carrots, scraped and diced

2 ribs celery, diced

1 to 2 leeks, dark green part only, rinsed thoroughly and sliced (optional)

2 large cloves garlic, peeled

1 bay leaf

2 sprigs fresh thyme, or $^{1}/_{2}$ teaspoon dried

10 stems parsley (optional)

$1^{1}/_{2}$ cups mushroom stems or sliced mushrooms (optional)

6 cups water

Pinch of salt (optional)

*Made of aromatic vegetables and herbs, vegetable stock is a delicious fat-free flavoring for casseroles. You can use canned vegetable broth, but homemade tastes better and is more economical, since you can make it from trimmings of carrots, onions, and celery. In addition, you can make your version much lower in sodium than commercial versions by using little or no salt.*

*Makes about 1 quart*

In a large saucepan, combine all the ingredients. Bring to a boil. Simmer, uncovered, over medium-low heat for 1 hour (45 minutes if you're in a hurry). Strain the stock into a large bowl, pressing on the vegetables to remove any excess moisture; discard the vegetables. Refrigerate or freeze the stock.

# INDEX

# About the Author

Award-winning author Faye Levy is crazy about casseroles. She loves time-honored classics like cassoulet, is passionate about paella, and counts homemade macaroni and cheese among her favorites.

In her cooking classes Faye teaches how to make tasty dishes that are nutritious and easy to prepare. Her students love her savory casseroles, such as her chicken with cumin and tomatoes, her eggplant curry, and her spiced lentils with rice. She enjoys using flavors from around the world and gets special inspiration from the Mediterranean region, where she lived for over twelve years.

Faye earned the "Grand Diplome" of the first graduating class of La Varenne Cooking School in Paris, where she studied and worked with the school's great chefs for six years. Upon returning to the United States, Faye became a columnist for *Bon Apétit* magazine, writing "The Basics" column for six years. She has contributed many fine recipes and articles to major national and international publications, including *Gourmet* magazine and *The Best of Gourmet* cookbook series.

*Faye Levy's International Vegetable Cookbook* won the James Beard Cookbook Award in 1994 as the best book in the category of fruits, vegetables, and grains. Faye also won cookbook awards from the International Association of Culinary Professionals for *Fresh from France: Vegetable Creations,* for *Classic Cooking Techniques,* and for *Sensational Chocolate.*

For the past seven years Faye has been a nationally syndicated columnist for the *Los Angeles Times* syndicate, focusing on quick, practical ways to cook delicious meals. Faye and her husband/associate Yakir Levy cook and write in Woodland Hills, California.